Berkley

FLAVORS *of* FISHING

C O O K B O O K

The Berkley *Flavors of Fishing Cookbook* is
brought to you by the manufacturers of
Trilene, America's #1 fishing line.

By Peggy Ramette and Dick Sternberg

CREDITS

Berkley— Flavors of Fishing Cookbook
Authors and Project Directors: Peggy Ramette, Dick Sternberg
Editor: Janice Cauley
Art Director: Lara Wyckoff
Home Economists: Ellen Meis, Peggy Ramette, Grace Wells

All recipes and preparation information in this book
  are excerpted from *America's Favorite Fish Recipes*
  from The Hunting & Fishing Library® and
  Microwave Cooking Library® published by
  Cy DeCosse Incorporated.

CONTENTS

6 | HOW TO FILLET FISH

8 | FRYING

18 | OVEN COOKING

32 | POACHING & STEAMING

40 | SIMMERING & STEWING

50 | GRILLING

60 | SMOKE COOKING

70 | PICKLING

76 | MICROWAVING

92 | INDEX

THE FLAVORS OF FISHING

Every angler knows—there are few fishing moments as exciting as the tap-tap-tap of a hungry walleye, the explosion of a wild-eyed bass from beneath your surface lure, the rise of a choosy brown trout to your mayfly imitation, or the deliberate dipping of your bobber as a palm-sized crappie sucks in your minnow.

And once the battle is over, there's always the satisfaction of cradling that beautiful fish in your wet hands as it rests in the water, and then watching it swim swiftly back home.

We at Berkley encourage the catch-and-release ethic. But we also know that "saving a few" for eating is a wonderful way to relive your trip later <u>and</u> have a truly superb meal. That's what *Flavors of Fishing* is all about—helping you make the most of the fish you decide to keep—from initial care and cleaning to cooking and serving your catch.

Thanks for purchasing America's Number One Fishing Partner—Super-Strong Berkley Trilene. I hope you enjoy <u>all</u> the great flavors of fishing this season!

Cheers,

Tom Bedell
Chief Executive Officer
Berkley Inc.

HOW TO FILLET FISH

Fishermen use a variety of filleting techniques. The method shown below is the easiest and quickest for most anglers. If your fillet board does not have a clip, you can use a fork to pin the head of a small fish. Salt on the hands helps hold a slippery fish.

The skin can be removed or left on. Fish such as largemouth bass have strong-tasting skin, so many anglers remove it. However, the skin on small trout and panfish is tasty. Panfish have large scales which must be removed if the skin is retained.

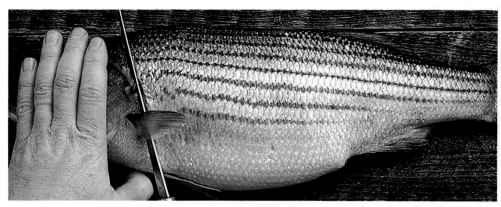

LIFT the pectoral fin. Angle the knife toward the back of the head and cut to the backbone.

TURN the blade parallel to the backbone. Cut toward tail with a sawing motion. Cut fillet off.

REMOVE the rib bones by sliding the blade along the ribs. Turn fish over and remove second fillet.

Keep the skin on fillets that will be charcoal grilled. This helps prevent the flesh from falling apart, sticking to the grill and overcooking. Cut long fillets into serving-size pieces before they are cooked or stored. To clean fillets, wipe with paper towels or rinse quickly under cold running water. Dry thoroughly with paper towels.

Save the bones and head after filleting. These pieces can be used for stock, chowder, fish cakes or other dishes.

CUT off the strip of fatty belly flesh. Discard guts and belly. Save bones and head for stock.

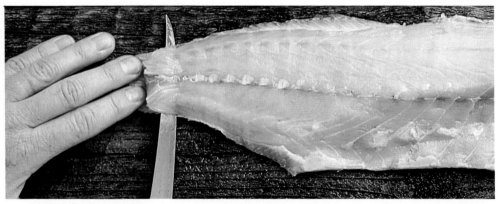

SKIN the fillet, if desired, by cutting into the tail flesh to the skin. Turn the blade parallel to the skin.

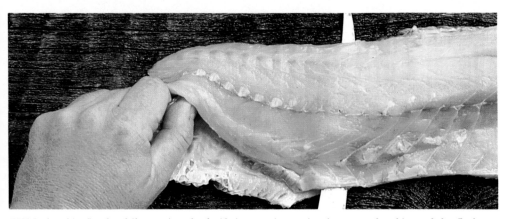

PULL the skin firmly while moving the knife in a sawing action between the skin and the flesh.

SALMON WITH FRESH TOMATO & BASIL

ELINOR KLIVANS — CAMDEN, MAINE   4 SERVINGS

3 tablespoons olive oil
4 salmon, or substitute, steaks
    (8 oz. each), 1 inch thick
1 cup coarsely chopped onions
2 cloves garlic, minced

1 tablespoon snipped fresh basil leaves
2 cups peeled seeded chopped tomatoes
1/4 cup water
1/4 teaspoon salt
1/4 teaspoon freshly ground pepper

In 10-inch skillet, heat oil over medium heat. Add steaks. Fry for 2 to 4 minutes, or until golden brown, turning over once. Remove steaks from skillet. Set aside.

To same skillet, add onions. Cook for 1 to 2 minutes, or until tender-crisp. Add garlic and basil. Cook for 1 minute. Stir in remaining ingredients.

Arrange steaks over tomato mixture. Reduce heat to low. Cover. Simmer for 11 to 13 minutes, or until fish is firm and opaque and just begins to flake. Serve over hot cooked linguine, if desired.

PER SERVING: CALORIES: 410; PROTEIN: 41 G.; CARBOHYDRATE: 8 G.; FAT: 23 G.;
CHOLESTEROL: 110 MG.; SODIUM: 233 MG.
EXCHANGES: 5 1/2 LEAN MEAT, 1 1/2 VEGETABLE, 1 FAT

PANFISH PARMESAN

CHRIS BROWN — OMAHA, NEBRASKA   6 SERVINGS

1/2 cup milk
1 egg, beaten
1 cup buttery cracker crumbs
1/2 cup grated Parmesan cheese

2 1/4 lbs. sunfish, or substitute, fillets
        (2 to 3 oz. each), skin removed
Vegetable oil

In medium mixing bowl, combine milk and egg. In shallow dish, combine crumbs and Parmesan cheese. Dip fillets first in milk mixture and then dredge in crumb mixture to coat.

In 12-inch skillet, heat 1/2 inch oil over medium heat. Add fillets. Fry for 4 1/2 to 6 minutes, or until golden brown, turning over once. Drain on paper-towel-lined plate.

PER SERVING: CALORIES: 479; PROTEIN: 37 G.; CARBOHYDRATE: 10 G.; FAT: 32 G.;
CHOLESTEROL: 122 MG.; SODIUM: 390 MG.
EXCHANGES: 2/3 STARCH, 5 LEAN MEAT, 3 1/2 FAT

BASS MARSALA

David L. Rehrig — Bethlehem, Pennsylvania   4 servings

 $^1\!/_3$ cup all-purpose flour
 $^1\!/_4$ teaspoon salt
 $1^1\!/_2$ lbs. bass, or substitute, fillets (6 oz. each),
     skin removed, cut in half crosswise
 2 tablespoons olive oil

 1 tablespoon margarine or butter
 $^2\!/_3$ cup Marsala wine
 $^1\!/_3$ cup snipped fresh parsley
 $^1\!/_8$ teaspoon dried oregano leaves

In shallow dish, combine flour and salt. Dredge fillets in flour mixture to coat. In 12-inch skillet, heat oil and margarine over medium heat until margarine is melted. Add fillets. Fry for 4 to 8 minutes, or until golden brown, turning over once.

Add Marsala, parsley and oregano to fish in skillet. Cook for 2 to 4 minutes, or until sauce is reduced by half, spooning sauce over fish frequently during cooking. Serve fish with sauce.

Per Serving: Calories: 380; Protein: 33 g.; Carbohydrate: 13 g.; Fat: 16 g.;
Cholesterol: 116 mg.; Sodium: 293 mg.
Exchanges: $^1\!/_2$ starch, $4^1\!/_2$ lean meat, $^1\!/_3$ fruit, $1^1\!/_2$ fat

CARAWAY RYE COATED FRIED FISH

WAYNE PHILLIPS — SASKATOON, SASKATCHEWAN   6 SERVINGS

2   eggs, beaten
$^1/_4$ teaspoon salt
$^1/_4$ teaspoon pepper
6   slices caraway rye bread, trimmed, dried
      and crumbled ($^3/_4$ cup)
1   tablespoon plus $1^1/_2$ teaspoons dried
      oregano leaves
$2^1/_4$ lbs. any freshwater fish fillets
      (6 oz. each), skin removed
      Vegetable oil

TOMATO SAUCE:
$^1/_2$ cup tomato sauce
2   tablespoons white wine or
      half-and-half
$^1/_2$ teaspoon sugar

In medium mixing bowl, combine eggs, salt and pepper. In shallow dish, combine bread crumbs and oregano. Dip fillets first in egg mixture and then dredge in crumb mixture to coat.

In 12-inch skillet, heat $^1/_8$ inch oil over medium heat. Add fillets. Fry for 5 to 8 minutes, or until golden brown, turning over once. Drain on paper-towel-lined plate.

In 8-inch skillet, combine sauce ingredients. Simmer over medium-low heat for 5 to 7 minutes, or until sauce is hot and slightly reduced. Spoon sauce over fish.

PER SERVING: CALORIES: 410; PROTEIN: 38 G.; CARBOHYDRATE: 16 G.; FAT: 21 G.;
CHOLESTEROL: 137 MG.; SODIUM: 440 MG.
EXCHANGES: 1 STARCH, $4^3/_4$ LEAN MEAT, $^1/_4$ VEGETABLE, $1^1/_4$ FAT

SOUTH LOUISIANA FISH FRY

KEN BECK — BATON ROUGE, LOUISIANA   6 SERVINGS

1 large green or red pepper, thinly sliced
   into rings
1 medium onion, cut in half lengthwise,
   then thinly sliced crosswise
1 cup seasoned coating mix

$2^1/4$ lbs. catfish, bass, or substitute, fillets
   (6 oz. each), skin removed,
   cut into $1^1/2$-inch pieces
   Vegetable oil

Heat oven to 175°F. Place half of pepper and onion slices into large paper grocery bag. Set aside. Place cornmeal mix in large plastic food-storage bag. Add fish, a few pieces at a time. Shake to coat.

In 10-inch skillet, heat $1/2$ inch oil over medium heat. Add half of fish. Fry for $3^1/2$ to 5 minutes, or until golden brown, turning over occasionally. With slotted spoon, remove fish from skillet. Place immediately into grocery bag. Hold bag closed. Shake gently. Add remaining pepper and onion slices to bag. Close bag. Repeat with remaining fish. Remove fish and vegetables from grocery bag and place in paper-towel-lined baking dish. Place in warm oven until ready to serve.

PER SERVING: CALORIES: 405; PROTEIN: 34 G.; CARBOHYDRATE: 16 G.; FAT: 22 G.;
CHOLESTEROL: 99 MG.; SODIUM: 945 MG.
EXCHANGES: 1 STARCH, $4^1/4$ LEAN MEAT, $1/2$ VEGETABLE, $1^3/4$ FAT

FISH CAKES

Thomas K. Squier — Aberdeen, North Carolina   3 servings

2 *cups any flaked cooked freshwater fish*	1 *teaspoon sesame oil (optional)*
1 *cup cornflake crumbs*	1/4 *teaspoon salt*
1/2 *cup sliced green onions*	1/4 *teaspoon pepper*
3 *eggs, divided*	1/2 *cup seasoned dry bread crumbs*
1 *tablespoon sherry*	2 *tablespoons vegetable oil*
1 *tablespoon Worcestershire sauce*	

In medium mixing bowl, combine fish, cornflake crumbs, onions, 1 egg, the sherry, Worcestershire sauce, sesame oil, salt and pepper. Divide mixture into 6 equal portions. Shape each portion into 1/2-inch-thick patties.

In small mixing bowl, lightly beat remaining 2 eggs. Place bread crumbs in shallow dish. Dip patties first in eggs and then dredge in crumbs to coat.

In 10-inch skillet, heat vegetable oil over medium heat. Add patties. Fry for 2 to 4 minutes, or until golden brown, turning over once. Drain on paper-towel-lined plate. Serve with lemon wedges, tartar sauce or cocktail sauce, if desired.

Per Serving: Calories: 543; Protein: 40 g.; Carbohydrate: 50 g.; Fat: 19 g.; Cholesterol: 289 mg.; Sodium: 1333 mg.
Exchanges: 3 1/3 starch, 4 lean meat, 1 1/2 fat

POTATO-FLAKED FILLETS

Vern Downey — Maple Heights, Ohio

6 SERVINGS

2/3 cup all-purpose flour
1 teaspoon paprika
1/4 teaspoon salt
1/4 teaspoon pepper
1/4 teaspoon garlic powder
1/4 teaspoon onion powder

2 eggs, beaten
2 cups instant potato buds or flakes
Vegetable oil
2 1/4 lbs. walleye, or substitute, fillets
(6 oz. each), skin removed

In shallow dish, combine flour, paprika, salt, pepper, garlic powder and onion powder. Place eggs in small mixing bowl. Place potato buds in second shallow dish. Dredge fillets first in flour mixture, then dip in eggs, and then dredge in potato buds to coat.

In 12-inch skillet, heat 1/4 inch oil over medium heat. Add fillets. Fry for 4 1/2 to 7 minutes, or until golden brown, turning over once. Drain on paper-towel-lined plate. Serve with lemon wedges and tartar sauce, if desired.

PER SERVING: CALORIES: 450; PROTEIN: 37 G.; CARBOHYDRATE: 23 G.; FAT: 22 G.;
CHOLESTEROL: 217 MG.; SODIUM: 214 MG.
EXCHANGES: 1 1/2 STARCH, 4 1/2 LEAN MEAT, 1 3/4 FAT

POTATO & ONION FRIED BASS

Roger D. Flanders — Gardnerville, Nevada

4 SERVINGS

1 1/2 lbs. bass, or substitute, fillets
(6 oz. each), skin removed,
cut in half crosswise
1/4 teaspoon pepper

1 1/2 cups instant potato buds or flakes
1 pkg. (1 oz.) dry onion soup mix
2 eggs, beaten
Vegetable oil

Sprinkle fillets evenly with pepper. In food processor or blender, combine potato buds and soup mix. Process until mixture is powdery. Place mixture in shallow dish. Place eggs in medium mixing bowl. Dredge fillets first in potato mixture, then dip in eggs, and then dredge in potato mixture to coat.

In 12-inch skillet, heat 1/8 inch oil over medium heat. Add fillets. Fry for 3 1/2 to 5 1/2 minutes, or until golden brown, turning over once. Drain on paper-towel-lined plate.

PER SERVING: CALORIES: 493; PROTEIN: 37 G.; CARBOHYDRATE: 18 G.; FAT: 30 G.;
CHOLESTEROL: 222 MG.; SODIUM: 804 MG.
EXCHANGES: 1 1/4 STARCH, 4 3/4 LEAN MEAT, 3 FAT

GREEN PEPPERCORN & RASPBERRY VINEGAR BASS

Rudy Liebl III — Fresno, California   4 SERVINGS

1/3 cup all-purpose flour

1 1/2 lbs. bass, or substitute, fillets
    (6 oz. each), skin removed,
    cut in half crosswise
    Vegetable oil

1 tablespoon vegetable oil

1/4 cup chopped shallots

1/2 cup ready-to-serve chicken broth

1/4 cup crème de cassis

3 tablespoons raspberry vinegar

1 tablespoon fresh lemon juice

1/2 cup brown sauce*

2 tablespoons brined green peppercorns,
    drained

Place flour in shallow dish. Dredge fillets in flour to coat. In 12-inch skillet, heat 1/8 inch oil over medium heat. Add fillets. Fry for 4 to 7 minutes, or until golden brown, turning over once. Remove fillets from skillet. Place on serving platter. Cover to keep warm. Set aside.

In 10-inch skillet, heat 1 tablespoon oil over medium heat. Add shallots. Cook for 1 1/2 to 2 minutes, or until tender. Stir in broth, crème de cassis, vinegar and juice. Bring mixture to a simmer. Reduce heat to medium-low. Simmer for 10 to 15 minutes, or until mixture is reduced by half, stirring occasionally. Add brown sauce and peppercorns. Simmer for 1 minute, or until hot, stirring constantly. Spoon sauce over fish.

*Brown sauce may be purchased in specialty stores or in the Oriental section of your supermarket.

PER SERVING: CALORIES: 546; PROTEIN: 34 G.; CARBOHYDRATE: 40 G.; FAT: 24 G.;
CHOLESTEROL: 116 MG.; SODIUM: 487 MG.
EXCHANGES: 3/4 STARCH, 4 1/2 LEAN MEAT, 1/2 FRUIT, 2 FAT

BAKED FISH FILLETS WITH HOT TOMATO SALSA

Vicki M. Lavorini — San Francisco, California   4 Servings

1½ lbs. *walleye, or substitute, fillets*
  (6 oz. each), skin removed
¼ teaspoon *salt*
¼ teaspoon *pepper*

1 can (16 oz.) *stewed tomatoes, drained*
¼ cup *hot or medium salsa*
3 tablespoons *tomato paste*

Heat oven to 400°F. Spray 11 x 7-inch baking dish with nonstick vegetable cooking spray. Arrange fillets, slightly overlapping, in prepared dish. Sprinkle evenly with salt and pepper. Set aside.

In small mixing bowl, combine tomatoes, salsa and tomato paste. Spoon mixture evenly over fillets. Cover dish with foil. Bake for 35 to 40 minutes, or until fish is firm and opaque and just begins to flake. Garnish with lemon wedges and serve over rice, if desired.

Per Serving: Calories: 202; Protein: 34 g.; Carbohydrate: 11 g.; Fat: 2 g.;
Cholesterol: 146 mg.; Sodium: 697 mg.
Exchanges: 3 lean meat, 2 vegetable

TROUT BAKED IN WINE

Peter R. Lebengood — Wyomissing, Pennsylvania   6 Servings

6 *whole drawn stream trout*
  (8 oz. each)
2 tablespoons *fresh lemon juice*
½ teaspoon *salt*

½ teaspoon *pepper*
½ cup *thinly sliced green onions*
2 tablespoons *snipped fresh parsley*
1 cup *Chablis or other dry white wine*

Heat oven to 400°F. Spray 13 x 9-inch baking dish with nonstick vegetable cooking spray. Set aside. Brush cavity of each trout evenly with juice. Sprinkle cavities evenly with salt and pepper.

Arrange fish in single layer in prepared dish. Sprinkle with onions and parsley. Pour wine evenly over fish. Bake for 25 to 30 minutes, or until fish begins to flake when fork is inserted at backbone in thickest part of fish, basting once or twice. Garnish with additional fresh parsley sprigs and lemon slices, if desired.

Per Serving: Calories: 165; Protein: 28 g.; Carbohydrate: 1 g.; Fat: 5 g.;
Cholesterol: 76 mg.; Sodium: 221 mg.
Exchanges: 3 lean meat

BAKED ALASKAN SALMON, HOMESTEADER-STYLE

STEVEN F. GRUBER — BEMIDJI, MINNESOTA

6 SERVINGS

1 whole drawn salmon or substitute (2 3/4 lbs.), head removed	1/2 cup finely chopped green pepper
1/2 teaspoon salt	1/2 cup finely chopped red pepper
1/4 teaspoon pepper	1/3 cup packed brown sugar
1 1/2 cups reduced-calorie mayonnaise	1/3 cup pickle relish
1 cup finely chopped onions	1/3 cup lemon juice
	1 teaspoon red pepper sauce

Heat oven to 325°F. Sprinkle cavity of fish evenly with salt and pepper. Cut 20 x 18-inch sheet of heavy-duty foil. Place in 13 x 9-inch baking dish, with ends hanging over. Place salmon in dish. Set aside.

In medium mixing bowl, combine remaining ingredients. Spoon some of mixture into cavity of fish. Spoon remaining mixture evenly over fish. Fold long sides of foil together in locked folds. Fold and crimp short ends; seal tightly. Bake for 1 hour to 1 hour 15 minutes, or until fish begins to flake when fork is inserted at backbone in thickest part of fish.

PER SERVING: CALORIES: 385; PROTEIN: 26 G.; CARBOHYDRATE: 24 G.; FAT: 21 G.; CHOLESTEROL: 84 MG.; SODIUM: 714 MG.
EXCHANGES: 3 1/2 LEAN MEAT, 1 VEGETABLE, 1 1/4 FRUIT, 2 FAT

SALMON WITH TARRAGON SAUCE

GEORGE GRUENEFELD — MONTREAL, QUEBEC   6 TO 8 SERVINGS

1   whole drawn salmon or substitute
     (3¹/₂ to 4¹/₂ lbs.), head removed
2   tablespoons snipped fresh parsley or
     1 teaspoon dried parsley flakes
1   tablespoon snipped fresh tarragon leaves
     or ¹/₂ teaspoon dried tarragon leaves
¹/₄ teaspoon salt
¹/₄ teaspoon paprika
¹/₈ teaspoon pepper
1   tablespoon fresh lemon juice

SAUCE:
¹/₄ cup margarine or butter
¹/₄ cup all-purpose flour
1   tablespoon snipped fresh tarragon leaves
     or ¹/₂ teaspoon dried tarragon leaves
¹/₂ teaspoon curry powder
¹/₄ teaspoon salt
¹/₈ teaspoon pepper
1   cup ready-to-serve chicken broth
1   cup milk
2   tablespoons dry white wine

Heat oven to 375°F. Cut 28 x 18-inch sheet of heavy-duty foil. Place salmon on foil. Sprinkle cavity and outside of fish with parsley, 1 tablespoon tarragon, ¹/₄ teaspoon salt and paprika, ¹/₈ teaspoon pepper and the juice. Fold long sides of foil together in locked folds. Fold and crimp short ends; seal tightly. Place on large baking sheet. Bake for 40 to 50 minutes, or until fish begins to flake when fork is inserted at backbone in thickest part of fish.

Meanwhile, prepare sauce. In 2-quart saucepan, melt margarine over medium heat. Stir in flour, tarragon, curry, salt and pepper. Blend in broth and milk. Cook over medium heat for 3 to 5 minutes, or until mixture thickens and bubbles, stirring constantly. Stir in wine. Serve salmon with sauce. Garnish with additional fresh tarragon sprigs, if desired.

PER SERVING: CALORIES: 233; PROTEIN: 22 G.; CARBOHYDRATE: 5 G.; FAT: 13 G.;
CHOLESTEROL: 59 MG.; SODIUM: 385 MG.
EXCHANGES: ¹/₃ STARCH, 3 LEAN MEAT, 1 FAT

OVEN-FRIED PIKE WITH ORANGE SAUCE

Gayetta Quenemoen — Great Falls, Montana

4 servings

$1^{1}/_{2}$ lbs. northern pike, or substitute, fillets
  (6 oz. each), skin removed,
  cut in half crosswise
1 cup orange juice
$1/_{4}$ cup thinly sliced green onions
2 tablespoons lemon juice

$1/_{4}$ cup vegetable oil, divided
$1/_{2}$ teaspoon ground ginger
$1/_{4}$ teaspoon salt
$1/_{2}$ cup all-purpose flour
1 tablespoon lemon herb seasoning

Place fillets in large plastic food-storage bag. Set aside. In 2-cup measure, combine orange juice, onions, lemon juice, 2 tablespoons oil, the ginger and salt. Reserve half of juice mixture. Cover and chill. Pour remaining juice mixture over fillets. Secure bag. Turn to coat. Chill $1/_{2}$ hour, turning bag once.

Pour remaining 2 tablespoons oil in 13 x 9-inch baking pan, tilting pan to coat bottom with oil. Heat oven to 450°F. Heat oil in oven for 10 to 15 minutes, or until very hot. In shallow dish, combine flour and lemon herb seasoning. Drain and discard juice mixture from fillets. Blot excess moisture from fillets with paper towels. Dredge both sides of fillets in flour mixture to coat. Place in hot oil in pan. Bake for 8 to 10 minutes, or until bottoms of fillets are browned. Turn fillets over. Bake for 5 to 6 minutes longer, or until browned on both sides.

Meanwhile, place reserved juice mixture in 1-quart saucepan. Simmer over medium heat for 10 to 12 minutes, or until reduced by half. Pour sauce over fillets. Garnish with orange slices and snipped fresh parsley, if desired.

Per Serving: Calories: 368; Protein: 35 g.; Carbohydrate: 22 g.; Fat: 15 g.;
Cholesterol: 66 mg.; Sodium: 208 mg.
Exchanges: $3/_{4}$ starch, $4^{1}/_{2}$ lean meat, $3/_{4}$ fruit, $1/_{4}$ fat

CARROT-TOPPED BAKED FISH

Ronald E. Fredrick — Algonquin, Illinois   4 servings

1½ lbs. any freshwater fish fillets (6 oz. each), skin removed	3 tablespoons margarine or butter
2 cups grated carrots	3 tablespoons plus 1½ teaspoons all-purpose flour
3 tablespoons margarine or butter, melted	¼ teaspoon salt
2 tablespoons lemon juice	¼ teaspoon pepper
¼ teaspoon ground thyme	⅓ cup milk
¼ teaspoon salt	

Heat oven to 450°F. Spray 13 x 9-inch baking dish with nonstick vegetable cooking spray. Arrange fillets, slightly overlapping, in prepared dish. Set aside.

In medium mixing bowl, combine carrots, melted margarine, juice, thyme and salt. Spread mixture evenly over fillets. Cover with foil. Bake for 25 to 35 minutes, or until fish is firm and opaque and just begins to flake. Drain liquid from fish into 2-cup measure. Cover fish with foil to keep warm. Set aside.

Add water to liquid in cup to equal 1⅓ cups. In 1-quart saucepan, melt 3 tablespoons margarine over medium heat. Stir in flour, salt and pepper. Blend in cooking liquid mixture and milk. Cook for 5 to 7 minutes, or until mixture thickens and bubbles, stirring constantly. Pour sauce evenly over fish. Garnish with sliced green onions and lemon slices, and serve over rice, if desired.

Per Serving: Calories: 376; Protein: 35 g.; Carbohydrate: 13 g.; Fat: 20 g.; Cholesterol: 149 mg. Sodium: 588 mg.
Exchanges: ½ starch, 4½ lean meat, 1 vegetable, 1¼ fat

CHEESY BAKED CATFISH

Virgil R. Meyer — Laverne, Oklahoma   6 servings

1 cup crushed cheese-flavored crackers	1/2 cup margarine or butter
1/4 cup sesame seed	2 1/4 lbs. catfish fillets (6 oz. each),
1 tablespoon snipped fresh parsley	skin removed
1/2 teaspoon salt	2 tablespoons shredded fresh Parmesan
1/4 teaspoon pepper	cheese
1/4 teaspoon cayenne	

Heat oven to 400°F. In shallow dish, combine crackers, sesame seed, parsley, salt, pepper and cayenne. Set aside.

In 1-quart saucepan, melt margarine over medium heat. Pour into another shallow dish. Dip each fillet first in margarine and then in crumb mixture, pressing lightly to coat.

Arrange fillets in single layer in 13 x 9-inch baking dish. Bake for 20 to 25 minutes, or until fish is firm and opaque and just begins to flake. Sprinkle fillets evenly with Parmesan cheese.

Per Serving: Calories: 447; Protein: 34 g.; Carbohydrate: 10 g.; Fat: 30 g.;
Cholesterol: 100 mg.; Sodium: 707 mg.
Exchanges: 3/4 starch, 4 1/2 lean meat, 3 1/4 fat

CHEESY WALLEYE BAKE

JULIE ZAK — EGG HARBOR, WISCONSIN   4 TO 6 SERVINGS

10 oz. fresh asparagus spears, cut into 1-inch pieces (2½ cups)	⅓ cup all-purpose flour
1½ lbs. walleye, or substitute, fillets (6 oz. each), skin removed	1 cup milk
¼ cup plus 2 tablespoons margarine or butter, divided	1⅓ cups shredded Cheddar cheese
1 medium onion, finely chopped (1 cup)	¼ teaspoon salt
	¼ teaspoon pepper
	1 cup crushed soda crackers

Heat oven to 350°F. Spread asparagus evenly over bottom of 10 x 6-inch baking dish. Arrange fillets, slightly overlapping, on top of asparagus. Set aside.

In 1-quart saucepan, melt 3 tablespoons margarine over medium-low heat. Add onion. Cook for 3 to 5 minutes, or until tender. Stir in flour. Cook for 2 minutes, stirring constantly. Blend in milk. Cook for 3 to 5 minutes, or until mixture thickens and bubbles, stirring constantly. Add cheese, salt and pepper. Remove from heat. Stir until cheese is melted. Spoon cheese sauce mixture evenly over fish fillets.

In 1-quart saucepan, melt remaining 3 tablespoons margarine over medium heat. Remove from heat. Add cracker crumbs, stirring to coat. Sprinkle crumb mixture evenly over cheese sauce. Bake for 40 to 45 minutes, or until sauce is hot and bubbly and fish is firm and opaque and just begins to flake. Let stand for 10 minutes before serving.

PER SERVING: CALORIES: 429; PROTEIN: 33 G.; CARBOHYDRATE: 20 G.; FAT: 24 G.;
CHOLESTEROL: 130 MG.; SODIUM: 587 MG.
EXCHANGES: 1 STARCH, 4 LEAN MEAT, ¼ SKIM MILK, 2½ FAT

ORIENTAL FISH BAKE

CHARLES E. NITSCHKE — NEW YORK MILLS, MINNESOTA   6 SERVINGS

1   tablespoon salt-free herb and spice blend
1   teaspoon onion powder
1   teaspoon garlic powder
1/2   teaspoon salt
1/4   to 1/2 teaspoon pepper
1/4   teaspoon cayenne

2   northern pike, or substitute, fillets
    (18 oz. each), skin removed
1   can (16 oz.) Oriental vegetables, rinsed
    and well drained
1/2   cup thinly sliced green onions
1/4   cup soy sauce

Heat oven to 325°F. Cut 20 x 18-inch sheet of heavy-duty foil. Place foil in 13 x 9-inch baking dish, with ends hanging over. Set aside.

In small bowl, combine seasonings. Sprinkle seasoning mixture evenly over one side of each fillet. Place 1 fillet seasoned-side-up in foil-lined dish. Top with Oriental vegetables and onions. Sprinkle with soy sauce. Place remaining fillet seasoned-side-up on vegetables.

Fold long sides of foil together in locked folds. Fold and crimp short ends; seal tightly. Bake for 40 to 45 minutes, or until fish is firm and opaque and just begins to flake.

PER SERVING: CALORIES: 179; PROTEIN: 35 G.; CARBOHYDRATE: 5 G.; FAT: 1 G.;
CHOLESTEROL: 66 MG.; SODIUM: 944 MG.
EXCHANGES: 4 LEAN MEAT, 1 VEGETABLE

CRISPY BAKED SALMON

Elinor Klivans — Camden, Maine 4 SERVINGS

1/4 cup ready-to-serve chicken broth or water	2 teaspoons grated lemon peel
2 lbs. salmon, or substitute, fillets (8 oz. each), skin on	1 tablespoon plus 1 teaspoon lemon juice
1/4 cup margarine or butter, melted, divided	1/4 teaspoon salt
1 cup unseasoned dry bread crumbs	1/4 teaspoon pepper
1/4 cup plus 2 tablespoons ground blanched almonds	1/4 cup sliced almonds

Heat oven to 375°F. Spray 11 x 7-inch baking dish with nonstick vegetable cooking spray. Pour broth into prepared dish. Arrange salmon fillets skin-sides-down in prepared dish. Set aside.

In medium mixing bowl, combine 1 tablespoon margarine, the bread crumbs, ground almonds, peel, juice, salt and pepper. Set aside.

Brush fillets with 1 tablespoon remaining margarine. Pat crumb mixture evenly on fillets. Drizzle with 1 tablespoon remaining margarine. Sprinkle almond slices evenly over crumb mixture.

Bake, uncovered, for 10 minutes. Drizzle with remaining 1 tablespoon margarine. Bake for 15 to 20 minutes, or until fish is firm and opaque and just begins to flake, and topping is golden brown.

Per Serving: Calories: 642; Protein: 52 g.; Carbohydrate: 23 g.; Fat: 37 g.;
Cholesterol: 126 mg.; Sodium: 617 mg.
Exchanges: 1 1/2 starch, 7 lean meat, 3 fat

CORNISH STRIPER PASTIES

Annette Bignami — Moscow, Idaho

6 servings

PASTRY:

4 1/2 cups all-purpose flour
1 teaspoon salt
1 teaspoon curry powder
1/4 teaspoon paprika
1 1/2 cups shortening
3/4 cup ice water

2 cups flaked cooked striped bass or substitute (about 1 lb.)
1 1/2 cups cubed red potatoes (1/4-inch cubes)
3/4 cup thinly sliced carrot

3/4 cup chopped onion
2 tablespoons plus 2 teaspoons sherry
1/2 teaspoon dried thyme leaves
1/8 teaspoon salt
1/8 teaspoon pepper
1 tablespoon all-purpose flour
1/2 teaspoon sugar
1 medium red or green cooking apple (8 oz.), cored and cut into 1/2-inch cubes

EGG WASH:

1 egg, beaten with 2 tablespoons water

In large mixing bowl, combine all pastry ingredients, except shortening and water. Cut in shortening to form coarse crumbs. Sprinkle with water, 1 tablespoon at a time, mixing with fork until particles are moistened and cling together. Form dough into ball. Wrap with plastic wrap. Chill 30 minutes.

Heat oven to 350°F. In another large mixing bowl, combine bass, potatoes, carrot, onion, sherry, thyme, salt and pepper. Set aside. In medium mixing bowl, combine 1 tablespoon flour and the sugar. Add apple. Stir to coat. Set aside.

Divide dough into 12 equal pieces. Place 2 pieces on lightly floured board. (Keep remaining pieces covered with plastic wrap.) Roll each piece to 7-inch-diameter circle. Place 1 scant cup of fish mixture on center of one circle, leaving 1-inch border. Top with 1/4 cup apple mixture.

Brush egg wash around edge of dough. Top with remaining dough circle. Press edges together with tines of fork to seal. Place pastry on ungreased baking sheet. Repeat with remaining dough, filling and apples. Bake for 40 to 45 minutes, or until crust is lightly browned.

PER SERVING: CALORIES: 974; PROTEIN: 29 G.; CARBOHYDRATE: 89 G.; FAT: 55 G.; CHOLESTEROL: 111 MG.; SODIUM: 500 MG.
EXCHANGES: 5 STARCH, 3 LEAN MEAT, 1/2 VEGETABLE, 1/2 FRUIT, 9 FAT

BAKED STUFFED TROUT

Mary B. Starinovich — Stafford Springs, Connecticut   4 servings

1/4 cup margarine or butter
1   small onion, chopped (3/4 cup)
1   stalk celery, chopped (1/2 cup)
2   slices bread, cut into 1/4-inch cubes
     (1 1/2 cups)
1   jar (4 1/2 oz.) sliced mushrooms, drained
1   dill pickle spear, finely chopped
     (1/4 cup)

1   tablespoon lemon juice
1   teaspoon dried parsley flakes
1/2 teaspoon salt
1/4 teaspoon dried basil leaves
1/8 teaspoon garlic powder
2   tablespoons vegetable oil
4   whole drawn stream trout (8 oz. each)

Heat oven to 350°F. In 10-inch skillet, melt margarine over medium heat. Add onion and celery. Cook for 3 to 5 minutes, or until tender. Remove from heat. Stir in remaining ingredients, except oil and trout. Set aside.

Pour oil into 13 x 9-inch baking dish. Roll each trout in oil to coat. Stuff each trout evenly with stuffing mixture. Arrange trout in single layer in prepared dish, spreading any additional stuffing mixture between trout. Bake for 25 to 30 minutes, or until fish begins to flake when fork is inserted at backbone in thickest part of fish.

Per Serving: Calories: 374; Protein: 30 g.; Carbohydrate: 11 g.; Fat: 23 g.;
Cholesterol: 77 mg.; Sodium: 796 mg.
Exchanges: 1/2 starch, 4 lean meat, 1/2 vegetable, 2 1/4 fat

COURT BOUILLON

1   leek, cut in half lengthwise and rinsed
4   sprigs fresh parsley
3   to 4 sprigs fresh thyme
1   large bay leaf
1   large clove garlic, cut in half

12   cups water
2   medium carrots, thinly sliced
2   ribs celery, thinly sliced
2   slices lemon

Prepare bouquet garni (seasoning bundle) as directed below. Set aside. Place water in stockpot or fish poacher. Add bouquet garni, carrots, celery and lemon. Cover. Bring to a boil over medium-high heat. Reduce heat to low. Simmer for 15 minutes. Add whole fish, fillets or steaks. Cook, covered, for 9 to 11 minutes per inch thickness, or until fish is firm and opaque and just begins to flake.

From outer layer of halved and rinsed leek, cut two 4-inch pieces. Wrap and refrigerate remaining leek for future use. Place parsley, thyme, bay leaf and garlic on concave side of 1 piece of leek. Cover with remaining piece of leek. Tie in 3 places with string to secure seasoning bundle.

NUTRITIONAL INFORMATION NOT AVAILABLE.

COCKTAIL PERCH

12   cups water
2   tablespoons salt
2   slices lemon

1   lb. yellow perch, or substitute, fillets
(2 to 3 oz. each), skin removed,
cut into 3 x $1/2$-inch strips
Crushed ice
Seafood cocktail sauce

In 6-quart Dutch oven or stockpot, combine water, salt and lemon. Bring to a boil over high heat. Reduce heat to medium. Add perch strips. Cook, uncovered, for 3 to 4 minutes, or until fish is firm and opaque and just begins to curl up. Lift fish strips from poaching liquid and plunge immediately into ice water. Leave fish in ice water until completely cooled. Serve fish strips on bed of crushed ice with cocktail sauce.

PER SERVING: CALORIES: 69; PROTEIN: 15 G.; CARBOHYDRATE: 0; FAT: 1 G.;
CHOLESTEROL: 68 MG.; SODIUM: 414 MG.
EXCHANGES: 2 LEAN MEAT

SALMON PASTA SALAD

VICKI J. SNYDER — COLUMBUS, OHIO   6 SERVINGS

2 salmon, or substitute, steaks
    (8 oz. each), 1 inch thick
1 recipe Court Bouillon, page 33
1 pkg. (12 oz.) uncooked mini lasagna
    noodles
1 cup thinly sliced carrots
1 tablespoon olive oil
1/2 cup thinly sliced celery
1/2 cup sliced green onions

1/2 cup chopped green pepper
1/4 cup pine nuts, toasted
1/2 cup mayonnaise
1/2 cup ranch salad dressing
1/4 teaspoon salt
1/8 teaspoon pepper
1 medium tomato, seeded and chopped
    (1 cup)
1/2 cup sliced black olives

Poach salmon in Court Bouillon as directed. Drain and discard poaching liquid. Chill salmon
2 hours. Remove skin and bones; flake meat. Set aside.

Prepare mini lasagna as directed on package, adding carrots to boiling water during last 1 minute
of cooking time. Rinse pasta and carrots with cold water. Drain. Place in large mixing bowl or salad
bowl. Add oil. Toss to coat. Add celery, onions, green pepper, salmon and pine nuts. Mix well.

In small mixing bowl, combine mayonnaise, ranch dressing, salt and pepper. Add mayonnaise
mixture to pasta mixture, stirring gently to coat. Serve immediately or cover and chill until
serving time. Top each serving evenly with tomatoes and olives.

PER SERVING: CALORIES: 623; PROTEIN: 23 G.; CARBOHYDRATE: 50 G.; FAT: 37 G.;
CHOLESTEROL: 53 MG.; SODIUM: 552 MG.
EXCHANGES: 3 STARCH, 2 LEAN MEAT, 1 VEGETABLE, 5 3/4 FAT

SALMON SALAD SANDWICHES

Vicki J. Snyder — Columbus, Ohio   4 to 6 servings

2   salmon, or substitute, steaks
     (8 oz. each), 1 inch thick
1   recipe Court Bouillon, page 33
2   hard-cooked eggs, chopped
1/2 cup mayonnaise
2   tablespoons sliced green onions
2   tablespoons sweet pickle relish

1   teaspoon lemon juice
1/2 teaspoon hot pepper sauce
1/4 teaspoon salt
1/8 teaspoon pepper
4   to 6 thick slices crusty bread
     Leaf lettuce

Poach salmon in Court Bouillon as directed. Drain and discard poaching liquid. Chill salmon 2 hours. Remove skin and bones; flake meat.

In medium mixing bowl, combine salmon and remaining ingredients, except bread and lettuce. Cover with plastic wrap. Chill about 1 hour. Serve on bread with lettuce.

Per Serving: Calories: 260; Protein: 16 g.; Carbohydrate: 3 g.; Fat: 21 g.;
Cholesterol: 118 mg.; Sodium: 292 mg.
Exchanges: 2 lean meat, 1/2 vegetable, 3 fat

WALLEYE ITALIANO

Ken and Donna White — Independence, Missouri　　　　　　　　4 to 5 servings

3 tablespoons margarine or butter	1/4 teaspoon dried oregano leaves
3/4 cup chopped onion	1/4 teaspoon pepper, divided
3/4 cup chopped green pepper	2 lbs. walleye, or substitute, fillets
1 cup tomato juice	(8 oz. each), skin removed
1 teaspoon chili powder	1 cup water
3/4 teaspoon salt, divided	1/2 cup white wine
1/4 teaspoon garlic powder	1 1/2 cups shredded mozzarella cheese
1/4 teaspoon dried thyme leaves	

Heat oven to 350°F. In 2-quart saucepan, melt margarine over medium-high heat. Add onion and green pepper. Cook for 4 to 5 minutes, or until vegetables are tender-crisp, stirring constantly. Stir in tomato juice, chili powder, 1/2 teaspoon salt, the garlic powder, thyme, oregano and 1/8 teaspoon pepper. Bring to a boil. Reduce heat to low. Simmer for 15 to 20 minutes, or until sauce thickens.

Meanwhile, place fillets in deep 10-inch skillet. Sprinkle with remaining 1/4 teaspoon salt and 1/8 teaspoon pepper. Pour water and wine over fish. Bring to a boil over medium-high heat. Reduce heat to low. Simmer, covered, for 8 to 10 minutes, or until fish is firm and opaque and just begins to flake.

Drain and discard poaching liquid. Place fillets in 11 x 7-inch baking dish. Spoon warm sauce over fish. Sprinkle evenly with cheese. Bake, uncovered, for 5 to 8 minutes, or until cheese is melted.

Per Serving: Calories: 353; Protein: 42 g.; Carbohydrate: 6 g.; Fat: 17 g.;
Cholesterol: 183 mg.; Sodium: 759 mg.
Exchanges: 5 1/2 lean meat, 1 vegetable

OVEN-POACHED WALLEYE

LORETTA CONKLIN — TUXEDO PARK, NEW YORK   6 SERVINGS

2¹/₄ lbs. walleye, or substitute, fillets   ¹/₄ teaspoon pepper
     (6 oz. each), skin removed   1¹/₂ cups milk
¹/₂ teaspoon salt   Sliced green onions
¹/₂ teaspoon paprika   Lemon wedges

Heat oven to 350°F. Place fillets in 13 x 9-inch baking dish. Sprinkle with salt, paprika and pepper. Pour milk over fish. Cover with foil. Bake for 30 to 35 minutes, or until fish is firm and opaque and just begins to flake.

Lift fillets from poaching liquid. Place on serving platter. Drain and discard poaching liquid. Before serving, sprinkle fish with onions and lemon juice.

PER SERVING: CALORIES: 147; PROTEIN: 29 G.; CARBOHYDRATE: 1 G.; FAT: 2 G.;
CHOLESTEROL: 131 MG.; SODIUM: 265 MG.
EXCHANGES: 4 LEAN MEAT

POACHED PANFISH
WITH LEMON CHIVE SAUCE

KEITH SUTTON — BENTON, ARKANSAS   4 SERVINGS

2   cups water
1   bay leaf
¼   teaspoon salt
2   tablespoons lemon juice
1½ lbs. yellow perch, or substitute, fillets
      (2 to 3 oz. each), skin removed

SAUCE:
⅓   cup margarine or butter
3   tablespoons snipped fresh chives
½   teaspoon grated lemon peel
¼   teaspoon salt
⅛   teaspoon pepper

In 10-inch skillet, combine water, bay leaf, ¼ teaspoon salt and the lemon juice. Bring to a boil over medium-high heat. Add fillets. Reduce heat to low. Simmer, covered, for 3 to 5 minutes, or until fish is firm and opaque and just begins to flake. Drain and discard poaching liquid. Cover fish to keep warm. Set aside.

In 8-inch skillet, melt margarine over medium heat. Add remaining sauce ingredients. Cook for 2 to 3 minutes, or until mixture is hot, stirring constantly. Serve sauce over fish.

PER SERVING: CALORIES: 292; PROTEIN: 33 G.; CARBOHYDRATE: 1 G.; FAT: 17 G.;
CHOLESTEROL: 153 MG.; SODIUM: 487 MG.
EXCHANGES: 4¾ LEAN MEAT, ½ FAT

NORTHWOODS MINESTRONE

2 tablespoons olive oil
1/2 cup sliced green onions
1/2 cup chopped red or green pepper
2 cans (28 oz. each) whole tomatoes,
   undrained and cut up
1/2 cup water
2 teaspoons sugar
1 teaspoon Italian seasoning
1/2 teaspoon salt
1/4 teaspoon garlic powder

1/8 to 1/4 teaspoon cayenne
1 1/2 lbs. walleye, or substitute, fillets
   (6 oz. each), skin removed, cut into
   1 1/2-inch pieces
1 can (15 1/2 oz.) dark red kidney beans,
   rinsed and drained
1 pkg. (9 oz.) frozen Italian or cut
   green beans
1 cup uncooked rotini

In 6-quart Dutch oven or stockpot, heat oil over medium-high heat. Add onions and chopped pepper. Cook for 3 to 5 minutes, or until vegetables are tender, stirring constantly.

Stir in tomatoes, water, sugar, Italian seasoning, salt, garlic powder and cayenne. Bring to a boil. Reduce heat to low. Simmer for 5 minutes.

Stir in remaining ingredients. Return mixture to a boil over medium-high heat. Reduce heat to low. Simmer for 15 to 20 minutes, or until fish is firm and opaque and just begins to flake, stirring occasionally.

PER SERVING: CALORIES: 242; PROTEIN: 21 G.; CARBOHYDRATE: 29 G.; FAT: 5 G.;
CHOLESTEROL: 61 MG.; SODIUM: 569 MG.
EXCHANGES: 1 STARCH, 2 LEAN MEAT, 2 VEGETABLE

WALLEYE & CLAM CHOWDER

DORIS M. BERGQUIST — FORT MOJAVE, ARIZONA   6 TO 8 SERVINGS

4   slices bacon, cut into $^1\!/2$-inch pieces
$^1\!/2$ cup thinly sliced celery
$^1\!/4$ cup sliced green onions
2   cups peeled cubed red potatoes
     (3 medium), $^1\!/2$-inch cubes
1   can (14$^1\!/2$ oz.) ready-to-serve
     chicken broth
$^1\!/2$ teaspoon dried dill weed
$^1\!/2$ teaspoon celery seed
$^1\!/4$ teaspoon salt

$^1\!/8$ teaspoon pepper
3   tablespoons all-purpose flour
3   cups milk
1$^1\!/2$ lbs. walleye, or substitute, fillets
     (6 oz. each), skin removed,
     cut into 1-inch pieces
1   cup whipping cream
1   can (6$^1\!/2$ oz.) minced clams, undrained
1   pkg. (10 oz.) frozen chopped spinach,
     defrosted and drained

In 6-quart Dutch oven or stockpot, cook bacon over medium heat until brown and crisp. Drain, reserving 2 tablespoons bacon drippings in Dutch oven. Set bacon aside.

Add celery and onions to bacon drippings in Dutch oven. Cook over medium-high heat for 3 to 5 minutes, or until vegetables are tender-crisp, stirring constantly. Stir in potatoes, broth, dill weed, celery seed, salt and pepper. Bring to a boil over medium-high heat. Reduce heat to low. Simmer, uncovered, for 10 to 15 minutes, or until potatoes are tender.

In 4-cup measure, combine flour and milk. Blend until smooth. Stir into broth mixture. Bring to a boil over medium-high heat. Reduce heat to low. Add walleye pieces. Simmer for 3 minutes, or until fish is firm and opaque and just begins to flake, stirring occasionally. Stir in bacon, cream, clams and spinach. Cook over low heat (do not boil) for 5 minutes, or until chowder is hot, stirring occasionally.

PER SERVING: CALORIES: 355; PROTEIN: 27 G.; CARBOHYDRATE: 17 G.; FAT: 20 G.;
CHOLESTEROL: 140 MG.; SODIUM: 507 MG.
EXCHANGES: $^1\!/2$ STARCH, 3 LEAN MEAT, $^1\!/2$ VEGETABLE, $^1\!/2$ SKIM MILK, 2$^1\!/4$ FAT

FISHERMAN'S CHOWDER

Marla Hart Clark — Moriarty, New Mexico

6 servings

- 1½ lbs. yellow perch, bass, or substitute, fillets (3 to 6 oz. each), skin removed, cut into 1-inch pieces
- ¼ cup all-purpose flour
- 2 tablespoons margarine or butter
- 2 cans (10¾ oz. each) condensed cream of mushroom soup
- 2 cups milk
- 2 cups peeled cubed red potatoes (3 medium), ½-inch cubes
- 1 cup chopped carrots
- 1 can (6 oz.) lump crabmeat, rinsed, drained and cartilage removed
- ½ cup chopped celery
- 1 tablespoon dried parsley flakes
- ½ teaspoon dried dill weed
- ½ teaspoon garlic powder
- ¼ teaspoon pepper

In shallow mixing bowl, combine perch pieces and flour. Toss gently to coat. In 6-quart Dutch oven or stockpot, melt margarine over medium-high heat. Add fish. Cook for 3 to 5 minutes, or until lightly browned, stirring constantly.

Add remaining ingredients. Bring to a boil over medium-high heat. Reduce heat to low. Simmer, uncovered, for 30 to 40 minutes, or until fish is firm and opaque and just begins to flake, stirring occasionally.

Per Serving: Calories: 391; Protein: 34 g.; Carbohydrate: 27 g.; Fat: 16 g.; Cholesterol: 140 mg.; Sodium: 1101 mg. Exchanges: 1½ starch, 4 lean meat, 1 vegetable, ¾ fat

PICANTE FISH CHOWDER

Vicki J. Snyder — Columbus, Ohio

6 servings

- 2 slices bacon, cut into ½-inch pieces
- 1 cup peeled cubed red potatoes, ½-inch cubes
- ½ cup chopped onion
- ½ cup chopped carrot
- ½ cup finely chopped zucchini
- ½ cup chopped celery
- ½ cup frozen corn
- 1½ lbs. yellow perch, bass, or substitute, fillets (3 to 6 oz. each), skin removed, cut into 1-inch pieces
- 2 cups water
- 1 can (14½ oz.) whole tomatoes, undrained and cut up
- ½ cup picante sauce
- 1 tablespoon Worcestershire sauce
- ¼ teaspoon salt
- ¼ teaspoon pepper
- Snipped fresh parsley

In 6-quart Dutch oven or stockpot, cook bacon over medium heat until brown and crisp. Add potatoes, onion, carrot, zucchini, celery and corn. Cook over medium-high heat for 3 to 5 minutes, or until vegetables are tender-crisp, stirring constantly.

Add remaining ingredients, except parsley. Bring to a boil over medium-high heat. Reduce heat to low. Simmer, uncovered, for 30 to 45 minutes, or until potatoes are tender, stirring occasionally. Sprinkle each serving evenly with parsley.

Per Serving: Calories: 238; Protein: 24 g.; Carbohydrate: 15 g.; Fat: 9 g.; Cholesterol: 82 mg.; Sodium: 504 mg. Exchanges: ½ starch, 3 lean meat, 1½ vegetable

DIXIE PANFISH CHOWDER

KEITH SUTTON — BENTON, ARKANSAS 4 SERVINGS

4 slices bacon
1/2 cup chopped onion
1/2 cup chopped carrot
1/4 cup chopped celery
1 lb. yellow perch, or substitute, fillets
(2 to 3 oz. each), skin removed, cut
into 1-inch pieces

1 can (16 oz.) whole Irish potatoes, rinsed,
drained and cut into 1/2-inch cubes
1 cup water
1/2 teaspoon salt
1/4 teaspoon pepper
1 cup milk
1 can (16 1/2 oz.) cream-style corn

In 6-quart Dutch oven or stockpot, cook bacon over medium heat until brown and crisp. Drain, reserving 2 tablespoons bacon drippings in Dutch oven. Crumble bacon. Set aside.

Add onion, carrot and celery to bacon drippings in Dutch oven. Cook over medium-high heat for 3 to 5 minutes, or until vegetables are tender-crisp, stirring constantly. Stir in perch pieces, potatoes, water, salt and pepper. Bring to a boil over medium-high heat. Reduce heat to low. Simmer, covered, for 8 to 10 minutes, or until fish is firm and opaque and just begins to flake.

Blend in milk and corn. Cook over medium heat (do not boil) for 5 to 7 minutes, or until mixture is hot, stirring occasionally. Sprinkle each serving evenly with crumbled bacon.

PER SERVING: CALORIES: 368; PROTEIN: 29 G.; CARBOHYDRATE: 38 G.; FAT: 12 G.;
CHOLESTEROL: 121 MG.; SODIUM: 852 MG.
EXCHANGES: 1 3/4 STARCH, 3 LEAN MEAT, 1/2 VEGETABLE, 1/4 SKIM MILK, 3/4 FAT

HEARTY CATFISH STEW

THOMAS K. SQUIER — ABERDEEN, NORTH CAROLINA 4 SERVINGS

2 cups peeled cubed red potatoes
(3 medium), 1/2-inch cubes
2 cups seeded chopped tomatoes
1 cup chopped onions
1 cup chopped green pepper
1 cup frozen corn
1 cup tomato juice
1 cup water

2 tablespoons margarine or butter
2 cloves garlic, minced
1/2 teaspoon salt
1/2 teaspoon dried thyme leaves (optional)
1/4 teaspoon pepper
1/8 to 1/4 teaspoon cayenne
4 catfish fillets (6 oz. each), skin removed,
cut into 1-inch pieces

In 6-quart Dutch oven or stockpot, combine all ingredients, except catfish pieces. Bring to a boil over medium-high heat. Reduce heat to low. Simmer, uncovered, for 10 to 12 minutes, or until potatoes are tender, stirring occasionally.

Add catfish. Simmer for 10 to 15 minutes, or until fish is firm and opaque and just begins to flake, stirring occasionally.

PER SERVING: CALORIES: 395; PROTEIN: 36 G.; CARBOHYDRATE: 33 G.; FAT: 14 G.;
CHOLESTEROL: 99 MG.; SODIUM: 684 MG.
EXCHANGES: 1 1/4 STARCH, 4 LEAN MEAT, 2 VEGETABLE, 1/4 FAT

CLIF'S HEARTY FISH CHOWDER

CLIF AND BETTY SANTA — VERMILION BAY, ONTARIO   8 SERVINGS

4 cups peeled cubed red potatoes
   (6 medium), 1/2-inch cubes
2 teaspoons salt
15 whole peppercorns
6 whole allspice
1/2 cup margarine or butter

1 can (12 oz.) evaporated milk
2 medium onions, thinly sliced
2 lbs. any freshwater fish fillets
   (8 oz. each), skin removed,
   cut into 2-inch pieces
3 tablespoons snipped fresh parsley

Place potatoes in 4-quart Dutch oven or stockpot. Add just enough water to cover potatoes. Bring to a boil over medium-high heat. Add salt, peppercorns and allspice. Cook for 3 to 5 minutes, or until potatoes are tender-crisp. Reduce heat to medium-low. Add margarine and milk. Stir until margarine is melted.

Layer onion slices over potatoes. Arrange salmon pieces on top of onions. Simmer (do not boil) for 20 to 30 minutes, or until fish is firm and opaque and just begins to flake and onions are tender, turning salmon pieces over once or twice. Sprinkle each serving evenly with parsley.

PER SERVING: CALORIES: 401; PROTEIN: 29 G.; CARBOHYDRATE: 20 G.; FAT: 23 G.;
CHOLESTEROL: 80 MG.; SODIUM: 800 MG.
EXCHANGES: 1 STARCH, 3 LEAN MEAT, 1/3 SKIM MILK, 2 3/4 FAT

BLUEGILLS BOUILLABAISSE
À LA JACK FROST

JACK FROST — ROUND LAKE, ILLINOIS

6 SERVINGS

1/4 cup olive oil
1 cup chopped onions
1 cup chopped red pepper
1 cup chopped green pepper
4 cloves garlic, minced
1 can (28 oz.) Roma tomatoes, undrained
    and cut up
1/4 cup port wine
1 bay leaf
2 teaspoons sugar

1/2 teaspoon salt
1/4 teaspoon saffron threads (optional)
1/8 teaspoon pepper
1 1/2 cups water
1 1/2 cups dry white wine
1 tablespoon lemon juice
2 lbs. sunfish, or substitute, fillets
    (2 to 3 oz. each), skin removed

In 6-quart Dutch oven or stockpot, heat oil over medium-high heat. Add onions, peppers and garlic. Cook for 3 to 5 minutes, or until vegetables are tender-crisp, stirring constantly.

Stir in tomatoes, port wine, bay leaf, sugar, salt, saffron and pepper. Bring to a boil over medium-high heat. Reduce heat to low. Simmer, uncovered, for 30 minutes. Stir in water, white wine and juice. Cook for 10 to 15 minutes, or until flavors are blended and mixture is hot.

Meanwhile, place sunfish fillets in large skillet. Add just enough water to cover fillets. Bring to a boil over medium-high heat. Reduce heat to low. Simmer for 3 to 4 minutes, or until fish is firm and opaque and just begins to flake. Drain and discard liquid. Add fillets to tomato mixture. Stir gently and cook over low heat until mixture is hot.

PER SERVING: CALORIES: 312; PROTEIN: 31 G.; CARBOHYDRATE: 13 G.; FAT: 11 G.;
CHOLESTEROL: 101 MG.; SODIUM: 525 MG.
EXCHANGES: 4 LEAN MEAT, 1 1/2 VEGETABLE, 1/2 FRUIT, 1/2 FAT

Berkley®
Trilene

Super Strong for Super Performance

TRIMAX

The ultimate high-performance fishing line. A revolutionary antifriction agent combines with advanced copolymer technology to deliver incredible abrasion resistance, outstanding castability and superior strength.

TRILENE XL

This extra-limp, small-diameter fishing line is Super Strong, with superior handling and knot strength.

TRILENE XT

Super Strong, tough and durable fishing line specially designed for the most rugged fishing conditions.

TRILENE XT SOLAR

Combines the strength and durability of XT with a unique solar collector additive that gives this line maximum visibility, to improve line control and help you detect strikes.

TRILENE ULTRATHIN

An extremely small-diameter line for light line fishing and finesse presentations.

TRILENE BIG GAME

Super Strong line with the muscle and shock-absorbing performance needed to handle big, powerful fish.

TRILENE COLD WEATHER

Super Strong line specially formulated to remain flexible in cold weather.

Berkley®
Trilene

America's #1 Fishing Line

CHARCOAL-GRILLED TROUT

RICHARD J. PARMLEY — ST. LOUIS, MISSOURI   2 SERVINGS

MARINADE:
- 1/4 cup olive oil
- 3 tablespoons fresh lemon juice
- 2 cloves garlic, minced
- 3 fresh basil leaves, finely snipped

- 1/8 teaspoon salt
- 1/8 teaspoon freshly ground pepper

- 2 whole drawn stream trout (8 oz. each)

In 11 x 7-inch baking dish, combine marinade ingredients. Place trout in baking dish, turning to coat. Brush some of marinade inside cavity of each fish. Cover with plastic wrap. Chill 2 hours.

Spray cooking grate with nonstick vegetable cooking spray. Prepare grill for high direct heat. Drain and discard marinade from fish.

Arrange trout on prepared cooking grate. Grill, covered, for 8 to 12 minutes, or until fish begins to flake when fork is inserted at backbone in thickest part of fish, turning over once. Garnish each serving with lemon and lime wedges, if desired.

PER SERVING: CALORIES: 299; PROTEIN: 29 G.; CARBOHYDRATE: 2 G.; FAT: 19 G.;
CHOLESTEROL: 80 MG.; SODIUM: 104 MG.
EXCHANGES: 4 LEAN MEAT, 1 1/2 FAT

FIESTA GRILLED FISH

PATRICIA M. SHORES — BINGHAMTON, NEW YORK   4 SERVINGS

- 1 whole drawn northern pike or substitute
  (2 to 3 lbs.), scaled, head removed
- 1/2 teaspoon salt
- 1/2 teaspoon pepper

- 1 small lemon, thinly sliced
- 1 small lime, thinly sliced
- 1 1/2 cups chunky salsa
- 1/2 cup beer

Prepare grill for low direct heat. Cut 2 sheets of 18-inch heavy-duty foil about 8 inches longer than fish. Sprinkle fish inside and out with salt and pepper. Place fish on 1 sheet of foil. Squeeze 1 slice each of lemon and lime over fish and stuff cavity with remaining slices. Fold sides and ends of foil up slightly around fish. Pour salsa and beer evenly over fish.

Fold long sides of foil together in locked folds. Fold and crimp short ends; seal tightly. Place packet on top of second sheet of foil. Overwrap by bringing long sides of foil together in locked folds. Twist short ends to seal, forming handles for turning packet.

Place packet on cooking grate. Grill, covered, for 15 minutes. Turn packet over. Grill, covered, for 15 to 18 minutes longer, or until fish begins to flake when fork is inserted at backbone in thickest part of fish.

PER SERVING: CALORIES: 185; PROTEIN: 31 G.; CARBOHYDRATE: 7 G.; FAT: 2 G.;
CHOLESTEROL: 137 MG.; SODIUM: 896 MG.
EXCHANGES: 4 LEAN MEAT, 1 1/2 VEGETABLE

POBLANO CATFISH IN LEEK

Mark S. Peniston — Irving, Texas

2 to 3 servings

2 leeks

1 medium red or green pepper, thinly sliced

1 poblano pepper (1 oz.), seeded and thinly sliced

3 tablespoons fresh cilantro leaves, chopped

2 cloves garlic, thinly sliced

2 small limes, thinly sliced

2 whole drawn catfish (about 1¼ lbs. each), head and skin removed

2 teaspoons prepared Cajun seasoning

Prepare grill for medium-high direct heat. Remove 4 large outer leaves from leeks. Set aside. Cut leeks in half lengthwise; rinse. Chop to equal 1 cup. In medium mixing bowl, combine chopped leeks, pepper slices, cilantro and garlic.

Spray 20-inch fish-grilling basket with nonstick vegetable cooking spray. On one side of basket, layer half of reserved leek leaves, half of lime slices and half of pepper mixture. Sprinkle both sides of each catfish evenly with Cajun seasoning. Arrange fish in basket. Top with remaining pepper mixture and lime slices. Cover with remaining leek leaves. Secure basket.

Place basket on cooking grate. Grill, covered, for 15 minutes. Turn basket over. Grill, covered, for 15 to 20 minutes longer, or until fish begins to flake when fork is inserted at backbone in thickest part of fish.

Per Serving: Calories: 243; Protein: 30 g.; Carbohydrate: 16 g.; Fat: 7 g.; Cholesterol: 90 mg.; Sodium: 671 mg.
Exchanges: 3 lean meat, 3 vegetable

BUTTERFLIED BARBECUED NORTHERN

THOMAS K. SQUIER — ABERDEEN, NORTH CAROLINA 6 SERVINGS

SAUCE:

- 1/4 cup tomato paste
- 2 tablespoons water
- 1 tablespoon fresh lime juice
- 1 tablespoon Worcestershire sauce
- 1 tablespoon molasses
- 1 1/2 teaspoons olive oil

- 1/2 teaspoon salt
- 1/8 teaspoon garlic powder

- 1 whole drawn northern pike, lake trout or substitute (3 1/2 to 4 1/2 lbs.), head and tail removed

Spray cooking grate with nonstick vegetable cooking spray. Prepare grill for medium direct heat. In small mixing bowl, combine sauce ingredients. Set sauce aside. Butterfly fish.

Place fish skin-side-down on prepared cooking grate. Grill, covered, for 5 minutes. Spread sauce evenly over fish. Grill, covered, for 6 to 10 minutes, or until fish is firm and opaque and just begins to flake. Garnish with snipped fresh chives and lime slices, if desired.

PER SERVING: CALORIES: 168; PROTEIN: 30 G.; CARBOHYDRATE: 5 G.; FAT: 2 G.;
CHOLESTEROL: 60 MG.; SODIUM: 357 MG.
EXCHANGES: 4 LEAN MEAT, 1 VEGETABLE

CATFISH MEXICANA

WILLIAM E. PUGH — CLEVELAND, OHIO   4 SERVINGS

1/2 cup milk
1/2 teaspoon ground cumin
1 1/2 lbs. catfish fillets (6 oz. each), skin
    removed
2 tablespoons olive oil
1 medium onion, finely chopped (1 cup)

1/2 cup chopped green, red or yellow pepper
1/4 cup snipped fresh cilantro leaves
1/4 teaspoon salt
1/4 teaspoon freshly ground pepper
4 teaspoons taco sauce or salsa (optional)

Combine milk and cumin in large, sealable plastic food-storage bag. Add fillets, turning to coat.
Seal bag. Chill 1 hour.

In 8-inch skillet, heat oil over medium heat. Add onion. Cook for 2 to 3 minutes, or until onion
is tender. Reduce heat to low. Stir in chopped pepper, cilantro, salt and pepper. Simmer,
uncovered, for 1 to 2 minutes, or until chopped pepper is tender-crisp. Set aside.

Prepare grill for high direct heat. Drain and discard milk mixture from fish. Cut four 14 x 12-inch
sheets of heavy-duty foil. Place 1 fillet on each sheet of foil. Top each fillet with one-fourth of
vegetable mixture and 1 teaspoon taco sauce. Fold long sides of foil together in locked folds.
Fold and crimp short ends; seal tightly.

Place packets on cooking grate. Grill, covered, for 11 to 17 minutes, or until fish is firm and
opaque and just begins to flake. Garnish with lemon and lime wedges, if desired.

PER SERVING: CALORIES: 290; PROTEIN: 33 G.; CARBOHYDRATE: 5 G.; FAT: 15 G.;
CHOLESTEROL: 101 MG.; SODIUM: 259 MG.
EXCHANGES: 4 LEAN MEAT, 1 VEGETABLE, 1/2 FAT

NORTHERN BEER BITES

Jim and Marianne Burke — Arlington, Texas   4 to 6 servings

   6 wooden skewers (10-inch)
Marinade:
   1/4 cup margarine or butter
   1 tablespoon olive oil
   4 to 5 cloves garlic, crushed
   1/4 teaspoon instant minced onion
   1/4 teaspoon snipped fresh dill weed

   1/4 teaspoon salt
   1/8 teaspoon freshly ground pepper

   1/2 cup beer
   2 northern pike, or substitute, fillets
      (12 oz. each), skin removed

Soak wooden skewers in water for 1/2 hour. In 1-quart saucepan, combine marinade ingredients. Cook over medium-low heat for 3 to 5 minutes, or until margarine is melted and mixture is hot, stirring occasionally. Remove from heat. Blend in beer. Set aside.

Cut each fillet lengthwise into three 10 x 1-inch strips. Thread 1 strip on each skewer, accordion-style. Arrange skewers in single layer in 11 x 7-inch baking dish. Pour marinade mixture over fish, turning skewers to coat. Cover with plastic wrap. Refrigerate 8 hours or overnight, turning over occasionally.

Spray cooking grate with nonstick vegetable cooking spray. Prepare grill for medium direct heat. Drain and discard marinade from fish. Arrange skewers on prepared cooking grate. Grill, covered, for 3 minutes. Turn skewers over. Grill, covered, for 2 to 3 minutes longer, or until fish is firm and opaque and just begins to flake. Serve with drawn butter and lemon wedges, if desired.

Per Serving: Calories: 151; Protein: 22 g.; Carbohydrate: 1 g.; Fat: 6 g.; Cholesterol: 44 mg.; Sodium: 137 mg. Exchanges: 3 lean meat

LEMONY APPLE-STUFFED SALMON

Kevin and Denise Greve — Goshen, Kentucky   4 servings

1   *whole drawn salmon or substitute*
    (2¹/₂ to 3 lbs.), head removed
1   *teaspoon dried dill weed*
1   *medium red cooking apple, cored and cut*
    into thin wedges

¹/₂   *medium onion, thinly sliced*
4   *thin lemon slices*
¹/₂   *cup margarine or butter, melted*

Build a campfire and allow it to burn down to glowing coals. Cut two 36 x 18-inch sheets of heavy-duty foil. Place salmon in center of 1 sheet. Turn up edges slightly. Sprinkle cavity of fish with dill. Stuff cavity of fish with apple, onion and lemon slices. Brush fish lightly with margarine. Pour remaining margarine over stuffing.

Fold long sides of foil together in locked folds. Fold and crimp short ends; seal tightly. Place packet seam-side-down on second sheet of foil. Fold as directed above. Place packet on cooking grate over campfire. Cook for 15 minutes. Turn packet over. Cook for 15 to 20 minutes longer, or until fish begins to flake when fork is inserted at backbone in thickest part of fish.

Per Serving: Calories: 492; Protein: 37 g.; Carbohydrate: 7 g.; Fat: 35 g.;
Cholesterol: 102 mg.; Sodium: 350 mg.
Exchanges: 3 lean meat, ¹/₃ fruit, 2¹/₂ fat

HOT WALDORF CRAYFISH

Thomas K. Squier — Aberdeen, North Carolina

2 servings

1 lb. cooked crayfish tails, in shell
2 medium red or green cooking apples, each
    cored and cut into 8 wedges

1/2 cup chopped pecans or walnuts
1/4 cup margarine or butter

Build a campfire and allow it to burn down to glowing coals. Cut four 18 x 14-inch sheets of heavy-duty foil. Place half of crayfish tails in center of each of 2 sheets of foil. Top each with half of apple wedges and pecans. Dot evenly with margarine.

Fold long sides of foil together in locked folds. Fold and crimp short ends; seal tightly. Place packets seam-side-down on remaining 2 sheets of foil. Fold as directed above. Place packets directly on coals. Cook for 4 minutes. Turn packets over. Cook for 3 to 5 minutes longer, or until apples are tender-crisp and mixture is hot.

Per Serving: Calories: 639; Protein: 39 g.; Carbohydrate: 26 g.; Fat: 44 g.;
Cholesterol: 271 mg.; Sodium: 371 mg.
Exchanges: 5 lean meat, 1 1/2 fruit, 5 3/4 fat

RIVERSIDE BULLHEADS

KEITH SUTTON — BENTON, ARKANSAS 3 SERVINGS

1 tablespoon margarine or butter, softened
6 whole drawn bullheads (4 to 6 oz. each),
     skin and heads removed
8 oz. fresh mushrooms, sliced (2 cups)
2/3 cup dry white wine
1/4 cup chopped onion
2 tablespoons vegetable oil

1 tablespoon plus 1 1/2 teaspoons dried
     parsley flakes
1 tablespoon plus 1 1/2 teaspoons fresh
     lemon juice
1/4 teaspoon salt
1/4 teaspoon freshly ground pepper
1/4 teaspoon dried thyme leaves

Build a campfire and allow it to burn down to glowing coals. Cut six 18 x 14-inch sheets of heavy-duty foil. Spread 1/2 teaspoon margarine on each sheet of foil. Place 1 bullhead in center of each sheet. Turn up edges slightly. In medium mixing bowl, combine remaining ingredients. Spread heaping 1/3 cup of mixture evenly over each fish.

Fold long sides of foil together in locked folds. Fold and crimp short ends; seal tightly. Place packets on cooking grate over campfire. Cook for 9 minutes. Turn packets over. Cook for 5 to 9 minutes longer, or until fish begins to flake when fork is inserted at backbone in thickest part of fish.

PER SERVING: CALORIES: 288; PROTEIN: 20 G.; CARBOHYDRATE: 5 G.; FAT: 17 G.;
CHOLESTEROL: 57 MG.; SODIUM: 293 MG.
EXCHANGES: 3 LEAN MEAT, 1 VEGETABLE, 1/4 FRUIT, 1 3/4 FAT

BLACKENED FISH

CLIF AND BETTY SANTA — VERMILION BAY, ONTARIO 6 SERVINGS

CAJUN SEASONING:
1 tablespoon paprika
2 1/2 teaspoons salt
1 teaspoon onion powder
1 teaspoon garlic powder
1 teaspoon cayenne
3/4 teaspoon white pepper

3/4 teaspoon black pepper
1/2 teaspoon dried thyme leaves, crushed
1/2 teaspoon dried oregano leaves

2 1/4 lbs. catfish, lake trout, or substitute,
     fillets (6 oz. each), skin removed,
     cut in half crosswise

Build a campfire and allow it to burn down to glowing coals. In shallow bowl, combine seasoning ingredients. Set aside. Place cast-iron skillet on cooking grate over campfire. When drop of water flicked onto skillet dances across it, skillet is hot. Dredge both sides of each fillet in seasoning mixture.

Squarely drop fillets into skillet. Cook for 2 minutes on each side, or until fish is firm and opaque and just begins to flake.

PER SERVING: CALORIES: 261; PROTEIN: 36 G.; CARBOHYDRATE: 2 G.; FAT: 11 G.;
CHOLESTEROL: 99 MG.; SODIUM: 1005 MG.
EXCHANGES: 5 LEAN MEAT

TROPICAL SMOKED SALMON

KATHLEEN D. BINGMAN — BENICIA, CALIFORNIA   4 SERVINGS

BRINE:

   2 *cups orange juice*
1¹/₂ *cups pineapple juice*
 ¹/₂ *cup water*
 ¹/₂ *cup packed brown sugar*
 ¹/₄ *cup canning or pickling salt*
 ¹/₄ *cup honey*

3 *tablespoons lemon juice*
1 *tablespoon lemon pepper*
1 *clove garlic, minced*

1 *lb. salmon, or substitute, fillets*
   (8 oz. each), 1 inch thick, skin on

In 5-quart glass or plastic container, combine brine ingredients. Stir until sugar and salt are dissolved. Add fillets to brine. Cover and refrigerate 12 hours or overnight.

Drain and discard brine from fillets. Rinse with water. Pat dry with paper towels. Arrange fillets on cooling racks. Air dry for 1 hour, or until fillets are shiny and dry.

Place oven thermometer in smoker. Heat dry smoker for 20 minutes, or until temperature registers 100°F. Spray smoker racks with nonstick vegetable cooking spray. Arrange fillets on prepared racks, spacing at least ¹/₂ inch apart.

Smoke fillets according to smoker manufacturer's directions (approximately 4 to 6 hours), or until fish is firm and opaque and internal temperature registers 180°F in thickest part of fillet, adding wood chips as necessary to impart desired flavor and to maintain desired level of smoke. Store smoked fish, loosely wrapped, in refrigerator no longer than 2 weeks. Serve with crackers.

PER SERVING: CALORIES: 379; PROTEIN: 45 G.; CARBOHYDRATE: 14 G.; FAT: 14 G.;
CHOLESTEROL: 125 MG.; SODIUM: 1704 MG.
EXCHANGES: 7 LEAN MEAT, 1 FRUIT

SMOKED SALMON

RON COTTERMAN — EAGLE RIVER, ALASKA   16 SERVINGS

BRINE:

   3 *cups water*
   3 *cups dry white wine*
   2 *cups soy sauce*
1²/₃ *cups sugar*
 ¹/₂ *cup canning or pickling salt*
 ¹/₂ *teaspoon garlic powder*

¹/₂ *teaspoon onion powder*
¹/₂ *teaspoon pepper*
¹/₂ *teaspoon red pepper sauce*

 8 *salmon, or substitute, steaks*
   (8 oz. each), 1 inch thick

In 5-quart glass or plastic container, combine brine ingredients. Stir until sugar and salt are dissolved. Add steaks to brine. Cover and refrigerate 12 hours or overnight.

Drain and discard brine from steaks. Rinse with water. Pat dry with paper towels. Arrange steaks on cooling racks. Air dry for 1 hour, or until steaks are shiny and dry.

Place oven thermometer in smoker. Heat dry smoker for 20 minutes, or until temperature registers 100°F. Spray smoker racks with nonstick vegetable cooking spray. Arrange steaks on prepared racks, spacing at least ¹/₂ inch apart.

Smoke steaks according to smoker manufacturer's directions (approximately 4 to 6 hours), or until fish is firm and opaque and internal temperature registers 180°F in thickest part of steak, adding wood chips as necessary to impart desired flavor and to maintain desired level of smoke. Store smoked fish, loosely wrapped, in refrigerator no longer than 2 weeks. Serve with thick slices of crusty French bread or crackers.

PER SERVING: CALORIES: 159; PROTEIN: 20 G.; CARBOHYDRATE: 4 G.; FAT: 6 G.;
CHOLESTEROL: 55 MG.; SODIUM: 998 MG.
EXCHANGES: 3 LEAN MEAT

CAPT. ANDY'S SUGAR-SMOKED WALLEYE

CAPT. ANDY EMRISKO — CLEVELAND, OHIO   12 SERVINGS

BRINE:

   8 cups apple juice
   3/4 cup canning or pickling salt
   1/4 cup packed brown sugar

   3 lbs. walleye, salmon, or substitute, fillets
     (8 oz. each), 1/2 to 1 inch thick, skin on

   4 to 6 cups cherry wood chips
   8 cups apple juice
   1/4 cup packed brown sugar

GLAZE:

   1/2 cup apple juice
   1 tablespoon packed brown sugar
   1 teaspoon honey

In 5-quart glass or plastic container, combine brine ingredients. Stir until salt and sugar are dissolved. Add fillets to brine. Cover and refrigerate 12 hours or overnight.

Place wood chips in large mixing bowl. Cover with water. Soak chips for 1 hour. Drain and discard brine from fillets. Rinse with water. Pat dry with paper towels. Arrange fillets on cooling racks. Air dry for 1 hour, or until fillets are shiny and dry.

Place oven thermometer in smoker. Add 8 cups apple juice and 1/4 cup brown sugar to water pan in smoker. Heat wet smoker with filled water pan for 20 minutes, or until temperature registers 100°F. Spray smoker racks with nonstick vegetable cooking spray. Arrange fillets on prepared racks, spacing at least 1/2 inch apart. Drain and discard water from wood chips.

Smoke fillets with wet chips according to smoker manufacturer's directions (approximately 2 to 3 hours), or until fish flakes easily with fork and internal temperature registers 180°F in thickest part of fillet.

In 1-quart saucepan, combine glaze ingredients. Cook over medium heat for 2 to 3 minutes, or until mixture is hot and sugar is dissolved, stirring frequently. Brush glaze over fillets. Continue smoking for 30 minutes to 1 hour, or until glaze is set. Store smoked fish, loosely wrapped, in refrigerator no longer than 2 weeks. Serve cold as an appetizer, or hot as a main dish.

PER SERVING: CALORIES: 134; PROTEIN: 22 G.; CARBOHYDRATE: 8 G.; FAT: 2 G.;
CHOLESTEROL: 98 MG.; SODIUM: 943 MG.
EXCHANGES: 3 LEAN MEAT, 1/2 FRUIT

SMOKED SALMON TRIANGLES

RUTH HOLCOMB — SPRING LAKE, NORTH CAROLINA 8 SERVINGS

1/2 cup margarine or butter, softened
2 tablespoons snipped fresh chives
1 tablespoon prepared horseradish
1/4 teaspoon garlic powder
1/4 teaspoon salt
8 slices dark rye or whole wheat bread

*6 to 8 oz. smoked salmon, or substitute,
    flaked (1 1/4 cups)*
*1 small tomato, cut into 8 thin slices
    Coarsely ground fresh pepper*
8 sprigs fresh dill weed

In small mixing bowl, combine margarine, chives, horseradish, garlic powder and salt. Spread about 1 tablespoon margarine mixture evenly on each slice of bread. Trim crusts from bread slices. Cut each slice in half diagonally to form triangles. Top each triangle evenly with flaked salmon. Cut tomato slices in half and place 1 half slice on each triangle. Sprinkle evenly with pepper. Garnish each triangle with sprig of dill.

PER SERVING: CALORIES: 202; PROTEIN: 8 G.; CARBOHYDRATE: 15 G.; FAT: 13 G.;
CHOLESTEROL: 6 MG.; SODIUM: 543 MG.
EXCHANGES: 1 STARCH, 2/3 LEAN MEAT, 2 FAT

HONEY-GLAZED SMOKED SALMON

JIM STACCHIOTTI — GIRARD, OHIO

8 cups water	3 lbs. salmon, or substitute, fillets
3/4 cup canning or pickling salt	(8 oz. each), 1 inch thick, skin
1/3 cup packed brown sugar	removed, cut into 3 x 4-inch pieces
1/2 teaspoon pepper	1/2 cup margarine or butter, melted
1/2 teaspoon onion powder	1 cup honey

In 5-quart glass or plastic container, combine water, salt, sugar, pepper and onion powder. Stir until salt and sugar are dissolved. Add salmon pieces to brine. Cover and refrigerate 8 hours or overnight.

Drain and discard brine from salmon. Rinse with water. Pat dry with paper towels. Arrange salmon pieces on cooling racks. Air dry for 1 hour, or until pieces are shiny and dry.

Heat oven to 350°F. Spray two 13 x 9-inch baking dishes with nonstick vegetable cooking spray. Arrange salmon pieces in single layer in each dish. In small mixing bowl, combine melted margarine and honey. Spoon honey mixture evenly over salmon in each dish. Bake for 20 to 30 minutes, or until fish is firm, basting once or twice. Cool slightly. Cover dishes with plastic wrap. Chill 3 hours.

Place oven thermometer in smoker. Heat dry smoker for 20 minutes, or until temperature registers 100°F. Spray smoker racks with nonstick vegetable cooking spray. Arrange salmon pieces on prepared racks, spacing at least 1/2 inch apart.

Smoke fillets according to smoker manufacturer's directions (approximately 1 1/2 to 3 hours), or until fish is firm and opaque and internal temperature registers 180°F in thickest part of fillet, adding wood chips as necessary to impart desired flavor and to maintain desired level of smoke. Store smoked fish, loosely wrapped, in refrigerator no longer than 2 weeks. Serve with crackers.

PER SERVING: CALORIES: 243; PROTEIN: 23 G.; CARBOHYDRATE: 13 G.; FAT: 11 G.;
CHOLESTEROL: 62 MG.; SODIUM: 894 MG.
EXCHANGES: 3 LEAN MEAT, 3/4 FRUIT, 1/2 FAT

SMOKED CARP RIBS

Jim Schneider — New Ulm, Minnesota   4 to 6 servings

1   whole drawn carp (12 lbs.),   ¹/2   cup canning or pickling salt
      head removed   1   small onion, thinly sliced
8   cups water

Fillet the fish, but do not remove the skin; cut off rib section (approximately 1 lb.) and remove belly meat. Rinse well. Reserve the rest of the meat for future use.

In 5-quart glass or plastic container, combine water and salt. Stir until salt is dissolved. Add ribs to brine. Cover and refrigerate 12 hours or overnight.

Drain and discard brine from ribs. Rinse with water. Pat dry with paper towels. Arrange ribs on cooling racks. Spread onion slices evenly over each rib portion. Air dry for 1 hour, or until ribs are shiny and dry.

Place oven thermometer in smoker. Heat dry smoker for 20 minutes, or until temperature registers 100°F. Spray smoker racks with nonstick vegetable cooking spray. Arrange ribs on prepared racks, spacing at least ¹/2 inch apart.

Smoke ribs according to smoker manufacturer's directions (approximately 4 to 6 hours), or until fish is firm and opaque and internal temperature registers 180°F in thickest part of ribs, adding wood chips as necessary to impart desired flavor and to maintain desired level of smoke. Cut between individual ribs to make serving-size pieces. Store smoked fish, loosely wrapped, in refrigerator no longer than 2 weeks.

Nutritional information not available.

SMOKED WHITEFISH

ROBERT C. REED — GROVER CITY, CALIFORNIA   8 SERVINGS

BRINE:

  6 *cups water*
$^2/_3$ *cup sugar*
$^1/_2$ *cup packed brown sugar*
$^1/_2$ *cup canning or pickling salt*
$^1/_3$ *cup soy sauce*

  2 *cloves garlic, crushed*
  1 *tablespoon pepper*
  2 *bay leaves, crushed*

  2 *lbs. whitefish, or substitute, fillets*
     (8 oz. each), $^1/_2$ inch thick, skin on

In 5-quart glass or plastic container, combine brine ingredients. Stir until sugar and salt are dissolved. Add fillets to brine. Cover and refrigerate 12 hours or overnight.

Drain and discard brine from fillets. Rinse with water. Pat dry with paper towels. Arrange fillets on cooling racks. Air dry for 1 hour, or until fillets are shiny and dry.

Place oven thermometer in smoker. Heat dry smoker for 20 minutes, or until temperature registers 100°F. Spray smoker racks with nonstick vegetable cooking spray. Arrange fillets on prepared racks, spacing at least $^1/_2$ inch apart.

Smoke fillets according to smoker manufacturer's directions (approximately 6 to 8 hours), or until fish is firm and opaque and internal temperature registers 180°F in thickest part of fillet, adding wood chips as necessary to impart desired flavor and to maintain desired level of smoke. Store smoked fish, loosely wrapped, in refrigerator no longer than 2 weeks. Serve with crackers.

PER SERVING: CALORIES: 177; PROTEIN: 22 G.; CARBOHYDRATE: 6 G.; FAT: 7 G.;
CHOLESTEROL: 68 MG.; SODIUM: 940 MG.
EXCHANGES: 3 LEAN MEAT, $^1/_2$ FRUIT

MARV'S GUIDE SERVICE
SECRET SMOKED FISH RECIPE

MARV McQUINN — HILLSBORO, OREGON   12 SERVINGS

BRINE:

  4 *cups water*
  2 *cups soy sauce*
  2 *cups apple juice*
  1 *cup packed brown sugar*
  $^1/_2$ *cup canning or pickling salt*
  2 *tablespoons whole black peppercorns*

1 *teaspoon garlic powder*
1 *teaspoon onion powder*
1 *teaspoon freshly ground pepper*

3 *lbs. lake trout, or substitute, fillets*
   (8 oz. each), 1 inch thick, skin on

In 5-quart glass or plastic container, combine brine ingredients. Stir until sugar and salt are dissolved. Add fillets to brine. Cover and refrigerate 12 hours or overnight.

Drain and discard brine from fillets. Rinse with water. Pat dry with paper towels. Arrange fillets on cooling racks. Air dry for 1 hour, or until fillets are shiny and dry.

Place oven thermometer in smoker. Heat dry smoker for 20 minutes, or until temperature registers 100°F. Spray smoker racks with nonstick vegetable cooking spray. Arrange fillets on prepared racks, spacing at least $^1/_2$ inch apart.

Smoke fillets according to smoker manufacturer's directions (approximately 6 to 8 hours), or until fish is firm and opaque and internal temperature registers 180°F in thickest part of fillet, adding wood chips as necessary to impart desired flavor and to maintain desired level of smoke. Store smoked fish, loosely wrapped, in refrigerator no longer than 2 weeks. Serve with crackers.

PER SERVING: CALORIES: 185; PROTEIN: 24 G.; CARBOHYDRATE: 4 G.; FAT: 8 G.;
CHOLESTEROL: 66 MG.; SODIUM: 870 MG.
EXCHANGES: 3 LEAN MEAT, $^1/_4$ FRUIT

TROUT SEVICHE

NORM AND SIL STRUNG — BOZEMAN, MONTANA

16 SERVINGS

1   lb. stream trout, or substitute, fillets
   (2 oz. each), skin removed
1   cup fresh key lime juice
1/4 cup minced jalapeño peppers
4   medium tomatoes, seeded and chopped
   (4 cups)

1   cup finely chopped red onion
1   cup thinly sliced celery
1/4 cup halved pimiento-stuffed green olives
1   teaspoon freshly ground black pepper
1   teaspoon salt

Freeze fish 48 hours at 0°F. Defrost. Cut into 1/2-inch pieces. Place fish in large glass or plastic bowl. Add juice and jalapeño peppers. Mix well. Add remaining ingredients, except salt, stirring gently to combine. With back of spoon, gently press mixture down into juices. Sprinkle salt evenly over top. Cover with plastic wrap. Chill 1 hour. Serve on toasted tortilla bits or crackers. Store in refrigerator no longer than 1 to 2 days.

PER SERVING: CALORIES: 56; PROTEIN: 7 G.; CARBOHYDRATE: 5 G.; FAT: 1 G.;
CHOLESTEROL: 16 MG.; SODIUM: 208 MG.
EXCHANGES: 3/4 LEAN MEAT, 1 VEGETABLE

PICKLED JACKS

BETTY R. WHITE — POLO, ILLINOIS

3 QUARTS

3   lbs. northern pike, or substitute, fillets
   (4 to 6 oz. each), skin removed
4   cups water
1   cup canning or pickling salt
8   cups distilled white vinegar, divided

1   large red or white onion, thinly sliced
2 1/2 cups sugar
1   tablespoon plus 1 teaspoon mustard seed
6   bay leaves
10 whole cloves

Freeze fish 48 hours at 0°F. Defrost. Cut into 1/2-inch strips. In large glass mixing bowl, combine water and salt. Stir until salt is almost dissolved. Add fish. Cover with plastic wrap. Refrigerate 2 days. Drain and discard brine. Rinse fish in cold water until rinse water is clear. Drain.

In same bowl, place fish and 4 cups vinegar. Cover with plastic wrap. Refrigerate 1 day. Drain and discard vinegar. Do not rinse fish. In three 1-quart jars, loosely layer fish and onion. Cover and chill.

In 2-quart saucepan, combine remaining 4 cups vinegar, the sugar and remaining ingredients. Bring mixture to a boil over medium-high heat, stirring constantly until sugar is dissolved. Reduce heat to medium-low and simmer for 15 minutes. Remove from heat. Cool completely. Pour pickling liquid over fish to cover. Seal jars, using two-part sealing lids. Refrigerate 1 week before serving. Store in refrigerator no longer than 4 weeks.

NUTRITIONAL INFORMATION NOT AVAILABLE.

EASY PICKLED NORTHERN

JAMES H. WRIGHT — MT. HOLLY, NEW JERSEY   3 PINTS

1¹/2 lbs. northern pike, or substitute, fillets
      (4 to 6 oz. each), skin removed, cut
      into 2 to 3-inch pieces
1   tablespoon plus 1¹/2 teaspoons mixed
      pickling spices

1   medium red onion, thinly sliced
3   slices lemon
1   quart distilled white vinegar
2   cups sugar

Heat oven to 325°F. Arrange fish in single layer in 13 x 9-inch baking dish. Sprinkle pickling spices evenly over fish. Top with onion and lemon slices. Pour vinegar over fish. Bake for 1 hour. Cool slightly. Cover with plastic wrap. Chill 4 hours, or until cold.

With slotted spoon, remove fish and onion from vinegar. Reserve vinegar. In three 1-pint jars, loosely layer fish and onion. Cover and chill. In 2-quart saucepan, combine reserved vinegar and the sugar. Bring mixture to a boil over medium-high heat, stirring constantly until sugar is dissolved.

Pour pickling liquid over fish to cover. Seal jars, using two-part sealing lids. Chill. Store in refrigerator no longer than 4 weeks.

NUTRITIONAL INFORMATION NOT AVAILABLE.

SWEET PEPPER PICKLED FISH

Thomas K. Squier — Aberdeen, North Carolina   2 QUARTS

2 to 3 lbs. any freshwater fish fillets	1½ cups sugar
(4 to 6 oz. each), skin removed	3 tablespoons mixed pickling spices
8 cups apple cider vinegar	½ cup chopped red pepper
¼ cup canning or pickling salt	1 large white onion, sliced

Freeze fish 48 hours at 0°F. Defrost. Cut into 1 to 2-inch pieces. Set aside. In large glass mixing bowl, combine vinegar and salt. Stir until salt is almost dissolved. Add fish. Cover with plastic wrap. Refrigerate 2 days.

With slotted spoon, remove fish from brine. Rinse fish with cold water until rinse water is clear. Reserve 3 cups brine. Cover and chill fish. Pour reserved brine into 4-quart saucepan. Add sugar, spices and red pepper. Bring mixture to a boil over medium-high heat, stirring constantly until sugar is dissolved. Remove from heat. Cool completely.

In two 1-quart jars, loosely layer fish and onion. Pour pickling liquid over fish to cover. Seal jars, using two-part sealing lids. Refrigerate 1 week before serving. Store in refrigerator no longer than 4 weeks.

NUTRITIONAL INFORMATION NOT AVAILABLE.

CREAMED SALMON

LYNN E. DEWITT — WEST OLIVE, MICHIGAN   3 QUARTS

3 1/2   lbs. salmon, or substitute, fillets   2   cups plus 2 tablespoons sugar, divided
           (8 oz. each), skin removed   1/4 cup mixed pickling spices
   3   to 4 medium onions, sliced   1/2 cup canning or pickling salt
   4   cups distilled white vinegar   1   carton (16 oz.) sour cream

Freeze fish 48 hours at 0°F. Defrost. Cut into 1 to 2-inch pieces. Set aside. In large glass mixing bowl, combine onions, vinegar, 2 cups sugar, the spices and salt. Stir until sugar and salt are almost dissolved.

Add fish. Cover with plastic wrap. Refrigerate 7 days, stirring mixture once every day. Drain and discard brine, reserving fish, onions and spices.

In large mixing bowl, combine sour cream and remaining 2 tablespoons sugar. Add fish mixture. Stir gently to coat. Loosely pack mixture into three 1-quart jars. Seal jars, using two-part sealing lids. Store in refrigerator no longer than 4 weeks.

NUTRITIONAL INFORMATION NOT AVAILABLE.

TROUT WITH WALNUT STUFFING

STUFFING:

2 tablespoons margarine or butter

2 tablespoons finely chopped celery

2 tablespoons sliced green onions

1 tablespoon snipped fresh parsley

1 cup herb-seasoned croutons

1/4 cup chopped walnuts

3 tablespoons ready-to-serve chicken broth
or water

1/4 teaspoon salt

1/4 teaspoon lemon pepper seasoning

1/8 teaspoon dried marjoram leaves

2 whole trout (6 to 8 oz. each),
heads removed

In 1-quart casserole, combine margarine, celery, onions and parsley. Cover. Microwave at High for 2 to 3 minutes, or until vegetables are tender-crisp. Add remaining stuffing ingredients. Mix well. Fill each trout with half of stuffing.

Arrange trout in 10-inch square casserole with backbones toward outside of casserole. Cover with wax paper. Microwave at 70% (Medium High) for 9 to 14 minutes, or until fish flakes easily when fork is inserted at backbone in thickest part of fish. Let stand, covered, for 2 to 3 minutes.

NUTRITIONAL INFORMATION NOT AVAILABLE.

POACHED TROUT WITH ONIONS & CAPERS

1 bottle (8 oz.) clam juice

3 tablespoons fresh lemon juice

1 small onion, thinly sliced, separated
into rings

1/2 teaspoon salt

1/4 teaspoon pepper

2 whole trout (6 to 8 oz. each),
heads removed

1/2 cup seasoned croutons, crushed

2 tablespoons margarine or butter

1 tablespoon capers, drained

1/8 teaspoon dried thyme leaves

Dash garlic powder

In 10-inch square casserole, combine clam juice, lemon juice, onion, salt and pepper. Cover. Microwave at High for 6 to 9 minutes, or just until mixture boils. Arrange trout in casserole with backbones toward outside of casserole. Re-cover. Reduce power to 70% (Medium High). Microwave for 6 to 9 minutes, or until fish flakes easily when fork is inserted at backbone at thickest part of fish, turning fish over after half the cooking time.

Place trout on serving platter. Top each trout with onion and croutons. Set aside. In 1-cup measure, combine margarine, capers, thyme and garlic powder. Microwave at High for 1 to 1 1/2 minutes, or until margarine melts. Spoon evenly over trout.

NUTRITIONAL INFORMATION NOT AVAILABLE.

JAPANESE MARINATED SALMON FILLETS

12- oz. salmon fillet, cut into 4 serving-size
   pieces

MARINADE:

2 tablespoons low-sodium soy sauce
1 tablespoon lemon juice
1 tablespoon packed brown sugar

1 clove garlic

1 leek (6 oz.), trimmed, cut in half
   lengthwise, rinsed, thinly sliced
1/2 cup julienne carrot
   (1 1/2 x 1/8-inch strips)

Arrange salmon fillets skin-sides-up in 8-inch square baking dish. Set aside.

In small mixing bowl, combine marinade ingredients. Stir to dissolve sugar. Pour mixture over
fillets, turning fillets to coat. Cover with plastic wrap. Chill 1 hour.

Turn fillets skin-sides-down. Sprinkle with leek and carrot. Re-cover with plastic wrap. Microwave
at 70% (Medium High) for 8 to 9 minutes, or until fish flakes easily with fork, rearranging pieces
twice. Serve with vegetables.

PER SERVING: CALORIES: 196; PROTEIN: 20 G.; CARBOHYDRATE: 12 G.; FAT: 7 G.;
CHOLESTEROL: 53 MG.; SODIUM: 374 MG.
EXCHANGES: 2 1/2 LEAN MEAT, 1 VEGETABLE, 1/2 FRUIT

COD FILLETS WITH CUCUMBER DILL SAUCE

1/2 medium cucumber, thinly sliced
1/4 teaspoon dill weed
2 green onions, chopped
1/4 teaspoon salt (optional)

1/2 cup plain low-fat yogurt
1 lb. cod fillets
2 teaspoons lemon juice

In food processor or blender, combine cucumber, dill, onions, salt and yogurt. Process until smooth. Pour into small bowl. Set sauce aside.

Arrange fish on roasting rack. Sprinkle with lemon juice. Cover with wax paper. Microwave at High for 5 to 7 minutes, or until fish flakes easily with fork, rearranging after half the cooking time. Set aside.

Reduce power to 50% (Medium). Microwave sauce for 1 to 3 minutes to heat. Serve over fish.

NUTRITIONAL INFORMATION NOT AVAILABLE.

JEAN'S FISH FILLETS

2 tablespoons margarine or butter
12 oz. flounder fillets, about 1/4 inch thick,
     cut into serving-size pieces
1/4 teaspoon salt
     Pepper
2 tablespoons finely chopped onion

2 tablespoons snipped fresh parsley
1 medium tomato, seeded and chopped
1/4 teaspoon dried basil leaves, optional
1/4 cup shredded Cheddar cheese
1/4 cup shredded Swiss cheese

Place mararine in 10-inch square casserole. Microwave at High for 45 seconds to 1 minute, or until melted. Add flounder, turning to coat.

Arrange flounder with thickest portions toward outside of casserole. Sprinkle with salt, pepper, onion, parsley, tomato and basil. Cover. Reduce power to 70% (Medium High). Microwave for 9 to 13 minutes, or until fish in center flakes easily with fork, rotating casserole once or twice.

NUTRITIONAL INFORMATION NOT AVAILABLE.

FILLETS WITH SWISS CHEESE SAUCE

4 to 6 servings

1/4 cup margarine or butter, *divided*
2 teaspoons dried parsley flakes, *divided*
1 teaspoon freeze-dried chives, *divided*
1 cup onion-garlic croutons, *crushed*
3 tablespoons all-purpose flour

1/4 teaspoon salt
1 cup milk
1/3 cup shredded Swiss cheese
1 lb. fish fillets, 1/2 inch thick, cut into
   serving-size pieces

In small mixing bowl, combine 2 tablespoons margarine, 1 teaspoon parsley and 1/2 teaspoon chives. Microwave at High for 45 seconds to 1 minute, or until margarine melts. Stir in crushed croutons until moistened. Set aside. Place remaining 2 tablespoons margarine in 2-cup measure. Microwave at High for 45 seconds to 1 minute, or until melted. Stir in flour, remaining 1 teaspoon parsley, remaining 1/2 teaspoon chives and the salt. Blend in milk. Microwave at High for 3 to 4 minutes, or until mixture thickens and bubbles, stirring well with whisk after every minute. Stir in cheese until melted. Set aside.

Arrange fish in 10-inch square casserole. Pour sauce over fillets. Cover with wax paper. Microwave at High for 4 to 6 minutes, or until fish flakes easily with fork, rearranging fish once. Sprinkle crouton mixture over fish. Microwave, uncovered, at 70% (Medium High) for 2 minutes.

To reheat: Place one serving on plate. Cover with wax paper. Microwave at High for 1 1/2 to 3 minutes, or until heated through.

Nutritional information not available.

LEMONY FILLETS & RICE

1 cup hot water
1/4 cup sliced green onions
2 tablespoons margarine or butter
1 tablespoon dried parsley flakes
1 tablespoon plus 1 teaspoon lemon juice, divided

1/2 teaspoon instant chicken bouillon granules
1 cup uncooked instant rice
1 pkg. (12 oz.) individually wrapped frozen fish fillets*
1/4 teaspoon dried thyme leaves

In 10-inch square casserole, combine water, onions, margarine, parsley, 1 tablespoon lemon juice and the bouillon. Microwave at High for 4 to 6 minutes, or until water boils. Stir in rice. Arrange frozen fillets on rice with thicker portions toward outside of casserole. Sprinkle remaining 1 teaspoon lemon juice on fish. Sprinkle with thyme. Cover. Microwave at High for 7 to 10 minutes, or until fish flakes easily with fork, rotating casserole once or twice. Fluff rice with fork before serving.

*If fillets cannot be separated, place on plate. Microwave at 50% (Medium) for 1½ to 2 minutes, or until easily separated, but still icy. Unwrap fillets.

To reheat: Place one serving on plate. Cover with wax paper. Microwave at High for 2 to 3½ minutes, or until heated through.

NUTRITIONAL INFORMATION NOT AVAILABLE.

STREAMED TROUT WITH WINE & LEMON

1 lb. trout fillets
4 slices lemon
1/4 cup white wine
1/4 cup chopped onion

1 teaspoon grated lemon peel
1/4 teaspoon pepper
1 teaspoon dried parsley flakes

Arrange fish in 12 x 8-inch baking dish. Top with lemon slices. In 1-cup measure, combine wine, onion, lemon peel, pepper and parsley. Pour over fish. Cover with wax paper. Microwave at High for 4 to 7 minutes, or until fish flakes easily with fork, rearranging after half the cooking time.

NUTRITIONAL INFORMATION NOT AVAILABLE.

ORANGE ROUGHY WITH KIWI-ORANGE SAUCE

SAUCE:
3/4 teaspoon cornstarch
1/3 cup orange juice
4 kiwifruit, peeled and sliced (24 slices), divided
2 teaspoons olive oil

1 teaspoon white wine vinegar

18 oz. orange roughy fillets, cut into 6 serving-size pieces
1/4 cup orange juice
1/2 teaspoon grated orange peel
6 orange slices

Place cornstarch in 2-cup measure. Blend in 1/3 cup orange juice. Microwave at High for 1 1/2 to 2 minutes, or until mixture is thickened and translucent, stirring once. Set aside.

In food processor or blender, place 12 kiwifruit slices, the oil and vinegar. Process until smooth. Pour into thickened orange juice mixture. Mix well. Set sauce aside.

In 10-inch square casserole, arrange orange roughy fillets in single layer. In 1-cup measure, combine 1/4 cup orange juice and the orange peel. Pour over fillets. Cover with wax paper. Microwave at High for 6 to 10 minutes, or until fish flakes easily with fork. Top each serving with 3 tablespoons sauce. Garnish with remaining kiwifruit slices and the orange slices.

PER SERVING: CALORIES: 171; PROTEIN: 13 G.; CARBOHYDRATE: 12 G.; FAT: 8 G.;
CHOLESTEROL: 17 MG.; SODIUM: 56 MG.
EXCHANGES: 2 LEAN MEAT, 1 FRUIT

SALMON SUCCOTASH SOUFFLÉ

$1/3$ cup chopped green pepper
$1/3$ cup chopped red pepper
  1 cup frozen corn
  2 tablespoons margarine or butter
$1/4$ cup all-purpose flour
$1/2$ teaspoon dried dill weed
$1/4$ teaspoon salt

$1/8$ teaspoon pepper
$1^1/2$ cups milk
  4 egg yolks, beaten
  1 can ($6^1/2$ oz.) skinless,
       boneless salmon, drained
  5 egg whites

Heat conventional oven to 350°F. Grease 2-quart soufflé dish. Set aside. In medium mixing bowl, combine chopped peppers, corn and margarine. Cover with plastic wrap. Microwave at High for 4 to 6 minutes, or until vegetables are tender, stirring once. Stir in flour, dill weed, salt and pepper. Blend in milk.

Microwave at High, uncovered, for 6 to $8^1/2$ minutes, or until mixture thickens and bubbles, stirring every 2 minutes. Stir small amount of hot mixture gradually into egg yolks. Blend yolks back into hot mixture. Add salmon. Mix well. Set aside.

In large mixing bowl, beat egg whites at high speed of electric mixer until stiff but not dry. Fold into salmon mixture. Pour mixture into prepared dish. Bake conventionally for 45 to 50 minutes, or until soufflé is golden brown and knife inserted in center comes out clean.

PER SERVING: CALORIES: 310; PROTEIN: 20 G.; CARBOHYDRATE: 21 G.; FAT: 16 G.;
CHOLESTEROL: 241 G.; SODIUM: 530 MG.
EXCHANGES: 1 STARCH, 2 MEDIUM-FAT MEAT, $1/2$ LOW-FAT MILK, $1/2$ FAT

SOLE FLORENTINE

2   pkgs. (10 oz. each) frozen chopped
    spinach
2   tablespoons dried minced onion
1/2 teaspoon grated lemon peel
1/2 teaspoon salt (optional)
1/2 teaspoon pepper

1/2 teaspoon dry mustard
2   tablespoons grated Parmesan cheese
1   teaspoon dried parsley flakes
1/2 teaspoon paprika
1   lb. sole fillets

Place spinach packages in oven. Microwave at High for 6 to 6½ minutes, or until packages flex easily. Rearrange once. Drain spinach well. Place in 8 x 8-inch square baking dish. Stir in onion, lemon peel, salt, pepper and mustard. Spread spinach mixture evenly over bottom of baking dish.

Combine Parmesan cheese, parsley and paprika. Set aside. Place fish on top of spinach mixture. Cover with wax paper. Microwave at High for 4 minutes. Rearrange and sprinkle with Parmesan mixture. Re-cover. Microwave at High for 2 to 6 minutes, or until fish flakes easily with fork.

NUTRITIONAL INFORMATION NOT AVAILABLE.

SOLE WITH HERBED VEGETABLES & RICE

1 SERVING

¹/3 cup uncooked instant brown rice
2 tablespoons water
¹/3 cup julienne carrot (2 x ¹/4-inch strips)
¹/3 cup julienne zucchini
(2 x ¹/4-inch strips)
¹/3 cup julienne yellow summer squash
(2 x ¹/4-inch strips)

1 sole fillet (about 4 oz.)
1 tablespoon margarine or butter
1 teaspoon grated lemon peel
¹/4 teaspoon Italian seasoning

Place rice on dinner plate. Sprinkle with water. Arrange vegetables over rice. Place sole fillet over vegetables. Set aside. In small bowl, microwave margarine at High for 45 seconds to 1 minute, or until melted. Add peel and Italian seasoning. Mix well. Drizzle margarine mixture over fish. Cover plate with plastic wrap. Microwave at High for 4 to 6 minutes, or until fish flakes easily with fork, rotating plate once. Pierce plastic wrap with tip of knife to release steam. Remove wrap. Before serving, fluff with fork.

NUTRITIONAL INFORMATION NOT AVAILABLE.

FISH WITH ZUCCHINI & RED PEPPER

$^{1}/_{4}$ cup finely chopped celery
$^{1}/_{2}$ cup finely chopped onion
$^{1}/_{2}$ cup shredded zucchini
1 tablespoon parsley flakes
2 tablespoons lemon juice

$^{1}/_{4}$ teaspoon black pepper (optional)
1 lb. fish fillets
1 small sweet red pepper, cut into thin
    strips

In small bowl, combine celery, onion, zucchini, parsley flakes, lemon juice and black pepper. Set aside.

Place fish fillets in 12 x 8-inch square baking dish. Top with vegetable mixture. Arrange red pepper strips over vegetables. Cover with wax paper. Microwave at 50% (Medium) for 10 to 15 minutes, or until fish flakes easily with fork, rearranging fillets once. Let stand, covered, for 2 to 3 minutes.

NUTRITIONAL INFORMATION NOT AVAILABLE.

HALIBUT WITH CREOLE RELISH

¼ cup chopped celery	¼ teaspoon dried basil leaves
¼ cup chopped green pepper	¼ teaspoon dried thyme leaves
¼ cup chopped onion	¼ teaspoon sugar
1 tablespoon plus 1 teaspoon lemon juice, divided	⅛ teaspoon salt
1 teaspoon vegetable oil	3 to 5 drops red pepper sauce
1 clove garlic, minced	½ cup seeded chopped tomato
½ teaspoon dried oregano leaves	2 halibut steaks (8 oz. each), about 1 inch thick

In 1-quart casserole, combine celery, pepper, onion, 1 teaspoon lemon juice, the oil, garlic, oregano, basil, thyme, sugar, salt and pepper sauce. Cover. Microwave at High for 3 to 4 minutes, or until vegetables are tender, stirring once. Stir in tomato. Set aside.

Cut bone from center of each halibut steak, using thin blade of knife and being careful not to slice all the way through ends of steaks. Cut each steak in half crosswise to yield 4 serving-size pieces.

In 8-inch square baking dish or on microwave roasting rack, arrange halibut steaks. Sprinkle with remaining 1 tablespoon lemon juice. Cover with wax paper. Microwave at 70% (Medium High) for 5 to 7 minutes, or until fish flakes easily with fork, rotating dish once or twice. Serve each halibut steak topped with about 3 tablespoons relish.

PER SERVING: CALORIES: 140; PROTEIN: 21 G.; CARBOHYDRATE: 5 G.; FAT: 4 G.;
CHOLESTEROL: 32 MG.; SODIUM: 133 MG.
EXCHANGES: 2½ LEAN MEAT, 1 VEGETABLE

MEDITERRANEAN FISH STEW

2 tablespoons olive oil

1 leek, thinly sliced, about $^3/_4$ cup

$^1/_2$ cup chopped green pepper

1 clove garlic, minced

$^1/_4$ teaspoon dried basil leaves

$^1/_4$ teaspoon turmeric

$^1/_8$ teaspoon fennel seed, crushed

1$^1/_2$ cups water

1$^1/_2$ cups tomato juice

$^1/_2$ cup sliced zucchini, $^1/_4$ inch thick

1 teaspoon instant vegetable bouillon
   granules

$^1/_2$ teaspoon sugar

$^1/_2$ teaspoon salt

2 slices orange

1 bay leaf

1 lb. cod fillets, about $^3/_4$ inch thick, cut
   into 1-inch pieces

In 2-quart casserole, combine oil, leek, green pepper, garlic, basil, turmeric and fennel. Cover. Microwave at High for 4 to 6 minutes, or until vegetables are tender, stirring once. Stir in remaining ingredients, except cod. Re-cover. Microwave at High for 10 to 15 minutes, or until zucchini is tender-crisp, stirring once. Remove orange slices and bay leaf. Gently stir in cod. Re-cover. Microwave at High for 3 to 4 minutes, or until fish flakes easily with fork, stirring after half the cooking time.

NUTRITIONAL INFORMATION NOT AVAILABLE.

ORANGE ROUGHY & CARROT SOUP

4 SERVINGS

8 oz. orange roughy fillets
2 tablespoons margarine or butter
3 cups thinly sliced carrots
1/4 cup chopped onion
1/4 teaspoon ground ginger

2/3 cup orange juice
1 can (14 1/2 oz.) ready-to-serve chicken
   broth
3/4 teaspoon salt
1/4 cup sliced green onions

Place orange roughy in 9-inch square baking dish. Cover with plastic wrap. Microwave at High
for 3 to 4 minutes, or until fish flakes easily with fork, turning fillets over after half the cooking
time. Set aside. In 2-quart casserole, combine margarine, carrots, chopped onion and ginger.
Cover. Microwave at High for 8 to 13 minutes, or until carrots are very tender, stirring every
2 minutes. In food processor or blender, combine carrot mixture and orange juice. Process
until smooth. Return mixture to 2-quart casserole. Stir in broth and salt. Cut orange roughy
into bite-size pieces. Stir into soup. Cover. Microwave at High for 3 to 7 minutes, or until
heated through, stirring gently every 2 minutes. Sprinkle each serving with green onions.

NUTRITIONAL INFORMATION NOT AVAILABLE.

HOT & SOUR FISH SOUP

1 pkg. (6 oz.) frozen pea pods	1 teaspoon packed brown sugar
4 cups water	1/2 teaspoon salt
1/2 cup chopped onion	1/4 teaspoon dried crushed red pepper
10 fresh mushrooms, cut in half	1/4 teaspoon grated lime peel
1 clove garlic, minced	3 tablespoons cornstarch
3 tablespoons white wine vinegar	3 tablespoons cold water
1 tablespoons soy sauce	12 oz. sole fillets, about 1/4 inch thick, cut
1 teaspoon instant chicken bouillon	into 1-inch pieces
granules	Shredded carrot (optional)

Unwrap pea pods and place on plate. Microwave at High for 2 minutes, or until defrosted. Set aside.

In 3-quart casserole, combine 4 cups water, the onion, mushrooms, garlic, vinegar, soy sauce, bouillon, sugar, salt, red pepper and lime peel. Cover. Microwave at High for 10 to 15 minutes, or until mixture boils.

In small bowl, blend cornstarch and water. Blend into hot mixture. Microwave, uncovered, at High for 5 to 10 minutes, or until mixture thickens and bubbles, stirring 2 or 3 times. Stir in pea pods and sole. Cover. Microwave at High for 2 to 3 minutes, or until fish flakes easily with fork. Garnish with shredded carrot.

NUTRITIONAL INFORMATION NOT AVAILABLE.

I N D E X

A

Appetizers,
Capt. Andy's Sugar-smoked
  Walleye, 63
Cocktail Perch, 33
Cornish Striper Pasties, 29
Creamed Salmon, 74
Easy Pickled Northern, 72
Honey-glazed Smoked Salmon, 65
Marv's Guide Service Secret
  Smoked Fish Recipe, 68
Northern Beer Bites, 55
Pickled Jacks, 71
Smoked Carp Ribs, 66
Smoked Salmon, 62
Smoked Salmon Triangles, 64
Smoked Whitefish, 67
Sweet Pepper Pickled Fish, 73
Tropical Smoked Salmon, 61
Trout Seviche, 71

B

Baked Alaskan Salmon,
  Homesteader-style, 20
Baked Fish Fillets with Hot Tomato
  Salsa, 19
Baked Stuffed Trout, 30

Baking, see: Oven Cooking

Bass,
Bass Marsala, 10
Fisherman's Chowder, 43
Green Peppercorn & Raspberry
  Vinegar Bass, 16
Picante Fish Chowder, 43
Potato & Onion Fried Bass, 15
South Louisiana Fish Fry, 12
See also: Recipes Using Any
  Freshwater Fish, Striped Bass
Bass Marsala, 10
Blackened Fish, 58

Bluegill,
Bluegills Bouillabaisse à la Jack
  Frost, 46
See also: Recipes Using Any
  Freshwater Fish, Sunfish
Bluegills Bouillabaisse à la
  Jack Frost, 46

Broiling, see: Oven Cooking

Bullhead,
Riverside Bullheads, 58
See also: Recipes Using Any
  Freshwater Fish
Butterflied Barbecued Northern, 53

C

Campfire Cooking,
Blackened Fish, 58
Hot Waldorf Crayfish, 57

Lemony Apple-stuffed Salmon, 56
Riverside Bullheads, 58
Capt. Andy's Sugar-smoked
  Walleye, 63
Caraway Rye Coated Fried Fish, 11

Carp,
Smoked Carp Ribs, 66
Carrot-topped Baked Fish, 23

Catfish,
Blackened Fish, 58
Catfish Mexicana, 54
Cheesy Baked Catfish, 24
Hearty Catfish Stew, 44
Poblano Catfish in Leek, 52
South Louisiana Fish Fry, 12
See also: Recipes Using Any
  Freshwater Fish
Catfish Mexicana, 54
Charcoal-grilled Trout, 51
Cheesy Baked Catfish, 24
Cheesy Walleye Bake, 25

Chowders, see: Soups
Cliff's Hearty Fish Chowder, 45
Cocktail Perch, 33
Cod Fillets with Cucumber
  Dill Sauce, 79

Cooked Fish, Recipes Using,
Cornish Striper Pasties, 29
Fish Cakes, 13
Salmon Salad Sandwiches, 35
Smoked Salmon Triangles, 64
Cornish Striper Pasties, 29
Court Bouillon, 33

Crayfish,
Hot Waldorf Crayfish, 57
Creamed Salmon, 74
Crispy Baked Salmon, 27

D

Dips, see: Appetizers
Dixie Panfish Chowder, 44

E

Easy Pickled Northern, 72

F

Fiesta Grilled Fish, 51

Fillets,
Baked Fish Fillets with Hot
  Tomato Salsa, 19
Bass Marsala, 10
Blackened Fish, 58
Bluegills Bouillabaisse à la
  Jack Frost, 46
Capt. Andy's Sugar-smoked
  Walleye, 63
Caraway Rye Coated Fried Fish, 11
Carrot-topped Baked Fish, 23

Catfish Mexicana, 54
Cheesy Baked Catfish, 24
Cheesy Walleye Bake, 25
Clif's Hearty Fish Chowder, 45
Cocktail Perch, 33
Cod Fillets with Cucumber Dill
  Sauce, 79
Creamed Salmon, 74
Crispy Baked Salmon, 27
Dixie Panfish Chowder, 44
Easy Pickled Northern, 72
Fillets with Swiss Cheese Sauce, 80
Fish with Zucchini & Red Pepper, 86
Fisherman's Chowder, 43
Green Peppercorn & Raspberry
  Vinegar Bass, 16
Hearty Catfish Stew, 44
Honey-glazed Smoked Salmon, 65
Hot & Sour Fish Soup, 90
Japanese Marinated Salmon
  Fillets, 78
Jean's Fish Fillets, 79
Lemony Fillets & Rice, 81
Marv's Guide Service Secret
  Smoked Fish Recipe, 68
Mediterranean Fish Stew, 88
Northern Beer Bites, 55
Northwoods Minestrone, 41
Orange Roughy & Carrot Soup, 89
Orange Roughy with Kiwi-Orange
  Sauce, 82
Oriental Fish Bake, 26
Oven-fried Pike with Orange
  Sauce, 22
Oven-poached Walleye, 37
Panfish Parmesan, 9
Picante Fish Chowder, 43
Pickled Jacks, 71
Poached Panfish with
  Lemon Chive Sauce, 38
Potato & Onion Fried Bass, 15
Potato-flaked Fillets, 15
Smoked Whitefish, 67
Sole Florentine, 84
Sole with Herbed Vegetables
  & Rice, 85
South Louisiana Fish Fry, 12
Steamed Trout with Wine &
  Lemon, 82
Sweet Pepper Pickled Fish, 73
Tropical Smoked Salmon, 61
Trout Seviche, 71
Walleye & Clam Chowder, 42
Walleye Italiano, 36
Fillets with Swiss Cheese Sauce, 80
Fish Cakes, 13
Fish with Zucchini & Red Pepper, 86
Fisherman's Chowder, 43

Flounder,
Jean's Fish Fillets, 79

Frying, 8-16,

Bass Marsala, 10
Caraway Rye Coated Fried Fish, 11
Fish Cakes, 13
Green Peppercorn & Raspberry
Vinegar Bass, 16
Panfish Parmesan, 9
Potato & Onion Fried Bass, 15
Potato-Flaked Fillets, 15
Salmon with Fresh Tomato &
Basil, 9
South Louisiana Fish Fry, 12
See also: Oven Cooking, Panfrying,
Stir-frying

G

Green Peppercorn &
Raspberry Vinegar Bass, 16

Grilling, 50-58

Butterflied Barbecued Northern, 53
Catfish Mexicana, 54
Charcoal-grilled Trout, 51
Fiesta Grilled Fish, 51
Northern Beer Bites, 55
Poblano Catfish in Leek, 52

H

Halibut with Creole Relish, 87
Hearty Catfish Stew, 44
Honey-glazed Smoked Salmon, 65
Hot & Sour Fish Soup, 90
Hot Waldorf Crayfish, 57

J

Japanese Marinated Salmon Fillets, 78
Jean's Fish Fillets, 79

L

Lake Trout,

Blackened Fish, 58
Marv's Guide Service Secret
Smoked Fish Recipe, 68
Poached Trout with Onions &
Capers, 77
See also: Recipes Using Any
Freshwater Fish
Lemony Apple-stuffed Salmon, 56
Lemony Fillets & Rice, 81

M

Marv's Guide Service Secret
Smoked Fish Recipe, 68
Mediterranean Fish Stew, 88

Microwaving, 76-90

Cod Fillets with Cucumber Dill
Sauce, 79
Fillets with Swiss Cheese Sauce, 80
Fish with Zucchini & Red Pepper, 86
Halibut with Creole Relish, 87
Hot & Sour Fish Soup, 90
Japanese Marinated Salmon
Fillets, 78
Jean's Fish Fillets, 79
Lemony Fillets & Rice, 81
Mediterranean Fish Stew, 88
Orange Roughy & Carrot Soup, 89

Orange Roughy with Kiwi-Orange
Sauce, 82
Poached Trout with Onions &
Capers, 77
Salmon Succotash Soufflé, 83
Sole Florentine, 84
Sole with Herbed Vegetables &
Rice, 85
Steamed Trout with Wine &
Lemon, 82
Trout with Walnut Stuffing, 77

N

Northern Beer Bites, 55

Northern Pike,

Butterflied Barbecued Northern, 53
Easy Pickled Northern, 72
Fiesta Grilled Fish, 51
Northern Beer Bites, 55
Oriental Fish Bake, 26
Oven-fried Pike with Orange
Sauce, 22
Pickled Jacks, 71
See also: Recipes Using
Any Freshwater Fish
Northwoods Minestrone, 41

O

Orange Roughy & Carrot Soup, 89
Orange Roughy with Kiwi-Orange
Sauce, 82
Oriental Fish Bake, 26

Oven Cooking, 18-30

Baked Alaskan Salmon,
Homesteader-style, 20
Baked Fish Fillets with
Hot Tomato Salsa, 19
Baked Stuffed Trout, 30
Carrot-topped Baked Fish, 23
Cheesy Baked Catfish, 24
Cheesy Walleye Bake, 25
Cornish Striper Pasties, 29
Crispy Baked Salmon, 27
Oriental Fish Bake, 26
Oven-fried Pike with Orange
Sauce, 22
Salmon with Tarragon Sauce, 21
Trout Baked in Wine, 19
Oven Frying, see: Oven cooking
Oven-fried Pike with Orange Sauce, 22
Oven-poached Walleye, 37

P

Panfish,

Panfish Parmesan, 9
Poached Panfish with
Lemon Chive Sauce, 38
See also: Recipes Using Any
Freshwater Fish
Panfish Parmesan, 9

Panfrying,

Bass Marsala, 10
Caraway Rye Coated Fried Fish, 11
Fish Cakes, 13
Green Peppercorn &
Raspberry Vinegar Bass, 16

Panfish Parmesan, 9
Potato & Onion Fried Bass, 15
Potato-flaked Fillets, 15
Salmon with Fresh Tomato &
Basil, 9
South Louisiana Fish Fry, 12

Pasta Dishes,

Salmon Pasta Salad, 34
Picante Fish Chowder, 43
Pickled Jacks, 71

Pickling, 70-74

Creamed Salmon, 74
Easy Pickled Northern, 72
Pickled Jacks, 71
Sweet Pepper Pickled Fish, 73
Trout Seviche, 71

Pike, see: Northern Pike

Poached Panfish with Lemon
Chive Sauce, 38
Poached Trout with Onions &
Capers, 77

Poaching & Steaming, 32-38,

Cocktail Perch, 33
Oven-poached Walleye, 37
Poached Panfish with
Lemon Chive Sauce, 38
Poached Trout with Onions &
Capers, 77
Salmon Pasta Salad, 34
Salmon Salad Sandwiches, 35
Walleye Italiano, 36
See also: Microwaving
Poblano Catfish in Leek, 52
Potato & Onion Fried Bass, 15
Potato-flaked Fillets, 15

R

Recipes Using Any
Freshwater Fish,

Caraway Rye Coated Fried Fish, 11
Carrot-topped Baked Fish, 23
Clif's Hearty Fish Chowder, 45
Fillets with Swiss Cheese Sauce, 80
Fish Cakes, 13
Fish with Zucchini & Red Pepper, 86
Lemony Fillets & Rice, 81
Pickled Fish, 92
Sweet Pepper Pickled Fish, 73
Riverside Bullheads, 58

S

Salmon,

Baked Alaskan Salmon,
Homesteader-style, 20
Creamed Salmon, 74
Crispy Baked Salmon, 27
Honey-glazed Smoked Salmon, 65
Japanese Marinated Salmon
Fillets, 78
Lemony Apple-stuffed Salmon, 56
Salmon Pasta Salad, 34
Salmon Salad Sandwiches, 35
Salmon Succotash Soufflé, 83

Salmon with Fresh Tomato &
  Basil, 9
Salmon with Tarragon Sauce, 21
Smoked Salmon, 62
Smoked Salmon Triangles, 64
Tropical Smoked Salmon, 61
See also: Recipes Using
  Any Freshwater Fish
Salmon Pasta Salad, 34
Salmon Salad Sandwiches, 35
Salmon Succotash Soufflé, 83
Salmon with Fresh Tomato & Basil, 9
Salmon with Tarragon Sauce, 21

Side Dishes & Salads,
Salmon Pasta Salad, 34
Salmon Salad Sandwiches, 35
See also: Pasta Dishes

Simmering & Stewing, 40-46
Bluegills Bouillabaisse à la Jack
  Frost, 46
Clif's Hearty Fish Chowder, 45
Dixie Panfish Chowder, 44
Fisherman's Chowder, 43
Hearty Catfish Stew, 44
Mediterranean Fish Stew, 88
Northwoods Minestrone, 41
Picante Fish Chowder, 43
Walleye & Clam Chowder, 42

Smoke Cooking, 60-68
Capt. Andy's Sugar-smoked
  Walleye, 63
Honey-glazed Smoked Salmon, 65
Marv's Guide Service Secret
  Smoked Fish Recipe, 68
Smoked Carp Ribs, 66
Smoked Salmon, 62
Smoked Whitefish, 67
Tropical Smoked Salmon, 61
Smoked Carp Ribs, 66
Smoked Salmon, 62
Smoked Salmon Triangles, 64
Smoked Whitefish, 67

Sole,
Sole Florentine, 84
Sole with Herbed Vegetables &
  Rice, 85
Sole Florentine, 84
Sole with Herbed Vegetables &
  Rice, 85

Soups,
Bluegills Bouillabaisse à la Jack
  Frost, 46
Clif's Hearty Fish Chowder, 45
Dixie Panfish Chowder, 44
Fisherman's Chowder, 43
Halibut with Creole Relish, 87
Hot & Sour Fish Soup, 90
Northwoods Minestrone, 41
Orange Roughy & Carrot Soup, 89
Picante Fish Chowder, 43
Walleye & Clam Chowder, 42
South Louisiana Fish Fry, 12

Spreads, see: Appetizers

Steaks,
Salmon Pasta Salad, 34
Salmon Salad Sandwiches, 35
Salmon with Fresh Tomato &
  Basil, 9
Smoked Salmon, 62
Steamed Trout with Wine &
  Lemon, 82

Steaming, see: Poaching & Steaming

Stewing, see: Simmering & Stewing

Stews,
Hearty Catfish Stew, 44
Mediterranean Fish Stew, 88

Stream Trout,
Baked Stuffed Trout, 30
Charcoal-grilled Trout, 51
Steamed Trout with Wine &
  Lemon, 82
Trout Baked in Wine, 19
Trout Seviche, 71
Trout with Walnut Stuffing, 77
See also: Recipes Using
  Any Freshwater Fish

Striped Bass,
Cornish Striper Pasties, 29
See also: Bass, Recipes Using
  Any Freshwater Fish

Sunfish,
Bluegills Bouillabaisse à la Jack
  Frost, 46
Panfish Parmesan, 9
See also: Panfish, Recipes
  Using Any Freshwater Fish
Sweet Pepper Pickled Fish, 73

T
Tropical Smoked Salmon, 61

Trout, see: Lake Trout, Stream Trout
Trout Baked in Wine, 19
Trout Seviche, 71
Trout with Walnut Stuffing, 77

W
Walleye,
Baked Fish Fillets with
  Hot Tomato Salsa, 19
Capt. Andy's Sugar-smoked
  Walleye, 63
Cheesy Walleye Bake, 25
Northwoods Minestrone, 41
Oven-poached Walleye, 37
Walleye & Clam Chowder, 42
Walleye Italiano, 36
See also: Recipes Using
  Any Freshwater Fish
Walleye & Clam Chowder, 42
Walleye Italiano, 36

Whitefish,
Smoked Whitefish, 67
See also: Recipes Using
  Any Freshwater Fish

Whole Fish,
Baked Alaskan Salmon,
  Homesteader-style, 20
Baked Stuffed Trout, 30
Butterflied Barbecued Northern, 53
Charcoal-grilled Trout, 51
Fiesta Grilled Fish, 51
Lemony Apple-stuffed Salmon, 56
Poached Trout with Onions &
  Capers, 77
Poblano Catfish in Leek, 52
Riverside Bullheads, 58
Salmon with Tarragon Sauce, 21
Trout Baked in Wine, 19
Trout with Walnut Stuffing, 77

Y
Yellow Perch,
Cocktail Perch, 33
Dixie Panfish Chowder, 44
Fisherman's Chowder, 43
Picante Fish Chowder, 43
Poached Panfish with
  Lemon Chive Sauce, 38
See also: Recipes Using
  Any Freshwater Fish

July. 2014

Cod in Coconut: Shaw's 350°
Soak loin in milk(or olive oil).
Roll in combination bread crumbs
and coconut flakes and
add salt & pepper.
Place in baker dish coated with
butter or oil. Dot w. butter.
Bake for 20 min. + until
done.

Enjoy your catch in even *more* delicious ways!

Hundreds of mouth-watering recipes, guaranteed delicious!

The taste-tempting recipes you see in *Flavors of Fishing* are just a sample of the ones you'll find in *America's Favorite Fish Recipes*. A handsome 8½" x 11", 160 page hardbound book filled with hundreds of photos, all color and over 175 recipes. It's a complete fish lovers collection, packed with step-by-step instructions on preparing entrees like Alder-Smoked Trout, Bass Picaso, Brandy-Barbecued Salmon Steaks, Honey-Fried Walleye Fillets and many more...*PLUS* dozens of tips on frying, poaching, steaming, stewing, oven cooking, grilling, smoking, pickling, even making soups and appetizers. You'll get nutritional information for each recipe to boot. *All for a special introductory price that makes it a great catch!*

ACT NOW SAVE $5 on *America's Favorite Fish Recipes*

America's Favorite Fish Recipes **is a great way to discover THE HUNTING & FISHING LIBRARY®**

The Hunting & Fishing Library® is a selection of books no outdoor enthusiast should be without. Volumes include *Largemouth Bass, Walleye, White-tailed Deer, Fishing Tips & Tricks,* and *Dressing & Cooking Wild Game.* Every book is filled with colorful photos and detailed information — everything you need to know to catch your limit, bag trophy game, and cook it all to perfection.

FREE TRIAL & FREE GIFT— ORDER TODAY!

Send in this postage-paid coupon for a **FREE 2-week** examination of *America's Favorite Fish Recipes*. If not totally satisfied, simply return it without obligation.

And get a **FREE GIFT** yours to keep with your **FREE TRIAL!** *Details on next page.* ⟶

Turn your favorite fish into an unforgettable dish.

If you thought the only way to cook fish is to fry them, *America's Favorite Fish Recipes* will open up a delicious new world of freshwater fish cookery.

THIS IS YOUR
FREE GIFT!

The illustrated 32-page booklet *101 Fishing & Hunting Secrets*. It will be yours to keep just for examining *America's Favorite Fish Recipes*.

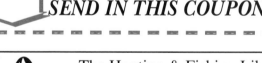

**Examine the complete hardcover edition of *America's Favorite Fish Recipes* for 2 weeks FREE!
ORDER TODAY and SAVE $5.00 off regular price.**

SEND IN THIS COUPON TODAY (or give it to a friend)!